DIVORCING A NARCISSIST:
THE ULTIMATE GUIDE TO END A DESTRUCTIVE MARRIAGE. HOW TO RECOVERY QUICKLY AND PROTECT YOURSELF FROM A TOXIC RELATIONSHIP

TABITHA MALONE

© **Copyright 2021 by Tabitha Malone - All rights reserved.**

The content contained within this book may not be reproduced, duplicated or transmitted without direct written permission from the author or the publisher.
Under no circumstances will any blame or legal responsibility be held against the publisher, or author, for any damages, reparation, or monetary loss due to the information contained within this book. Either directly or indirectly.

Legal Notice:
This book is copyright protected. This book is only for personal use. You cannot amend, distribute, sell, use, quote or paraphrase any part, or the content within this book, without the consent of the author or publisher.

Disclaimer Notice:
Please note the information contained within this document is for educational and entertainment purposes only. All effort has been executed to present accurate, up to date, and reliable, complete information. No warranties of any kind are declared or implied. Readers acknowledge that the author is not engaging in the rendering of legal, financial, medical or professional advice. The content within this book has been derived from various sources. Please consult a licensed professional before attempting any techniques outlined in this book.
By reading this document, the reader agrees that under no circumstances is the author responsible for any losses, direct or indirect, which are incurred as a result of the use of information contained within this document, including, but not limited to, — errors, omissions, or inaccuracies.

Table of Contents

Introduction 6

1) Why Are Narcissists So Attractive? 11
2) Having A Relationship with A Narcissist 15
3) Getting Married to a Narcissist 21
4) Why Is A Narcissist Getting Married? 25
5) Narcissist Betrayals 31
6) The Violence/Cruelty of a Narcissist in Marriage 36
7) Stuck In A Relationship With A Narcissist 40
8) Having Children in the Narcissistic Relationship 46
9) Ending A Relationship with A Narcissist 52
10) Divorcing a Narcissist 57
11) Do Not Change Your Mind and Remember your Motivation 62
12) Division of Finance 65
13) Dealing with Co-Parenting with a Narcissist 69
14) How to Protect Your Children From A Violent Narcissistic Father 74
15) The Psychological Consequences After A Toxic Relationship 79
16) Lasting Effects 84
17) Trauma Bond 89
18) Avoid Repeating Errors after Leaving in a Toxic Relationship 94
19) Professional and Medical advice from Narcissistic Abuse 99
20) Your Road to Recovery 103

21) Allowing Yourself to Be Who You Are.. 108

22) Loving Again.. 114

   Conclusion 120

Introduction

Due to the amount of control a narcissist tends to have over our lives, many people understandably feel lost and a bit unsure of how to navigate their life after being with a narcissist.

That is, unfortunately, part of the control they have over us. They feed off our insecurity, how unsure we often feel, and then use that insecurity against us. These people often alienate us from anybody in our support network to the point where the narcissist is all we have, and their worldview dominates the proverbial conversation.

Control is paramount to a narcissist. Unfortunately, they often find themselves attracted to low self-esteem, who feel like they have no control over their destiny. In one or another, it is the perfect combination – the narcissist needs to control, and their victims often have no experience outside of being controlled.

The problem is, this is an unhealthy dynamic that reduces the victim to a shell of a person and often leaves them alone, with no self-confidence and at a loss for how they should navigate the world.

The hardest thing about rebuilding your life after divorcing your narcissist ex forgives yourself for allowing it to happen. It is incredibly common for people to blame themselves.

They feel like they should have seen the red flags or been more vital to have left earlier. All of these things are ways of deflecting the blame from where it belongs: on the narcissist.

A lot of highly intelligent people fall prey to this behavior due to the insidious nature of narcissism. It is not a character flaw to fall victim to a narcissist's charms.

Narcissists are keen manipulators and are excellent on how to get what they want from people. They know what they are doing and often really, really good at it.

The types of people they prey on are chosen for a reason. Their victim is already in a low place, and the narcissist swoops in and often acts like a knight in shining armor or offers to take control of the proverbial ship.

It also takes time to get over a toxic relationship like this. The recovery process goes far beyond not going back to the narcissist and forgiving yourself for being, well, human. These relationships do a lot of untold damage to people. They leave them jaded, unable to trust, perhaps even unwilling to attempt connections again for fear of repeating the same experience.

While it is essential to give yourself time before you jump back into dating, you need to allow yourself to go through grief stages, but you also do not want to wallow in it. It is a good time to rebuild your support network, which will be vital for you in the long-term.

It does need to be considered that, while you shouldn't blame yourself for ending up in a relationship with a narcissist and having trouble getting out of a said relationship, there are important lessons that need to be learned from your experience.

Suppose you fail to look back critically on the relationship to see where the red flags were, where things took an unpleasant twist. You will likely end up in a similarly unhappy relationship in the future.

It is not at all to blame the victim. That is what someone who has survived a relationship with a narcissist is: a victim. But there are lessons to be learned, and there are things that you will need to look for and protect yourself against. So, you aren't a victim again and again.

The sad reality is that people who are often drawn to the narcissist end up with very similar partners throughout their lives, which is incredibly unfortunate. It is toxic to their very sense of self. These victims often need a support network that provides perspective and helps to stay strong in the future.

Having a broad coalition of friends and family will help keep your level and give you the strength you need to make better relationship choices. Also, to learn how to spot the signs that somebody is toxic before getting too deep with them.

Another thing that also needs to be touched upon is that the rebuilding process is complicated for children with their narcissistic ex.

With children, complete disengagement from the narcissist isn't just usually an option. It makes the entire dynamic a lot more volatile and trickier to navigate. If you're in this situation, here are few things to help keep things as civil as possible and keep the conversation to support the children.

Though it is not ideal, there are many cases where it is best to have a neutral third party mediate between you and the narcissistic other. This way, they cannot manipulate you or pull any of the tricks used against you in the past. When there are mediators, things tend to be a lot more civil and respectful, as the exes do not speak directly to each other.

If you feel that the narcissist is dangerous or unhealthy for the child to be around, bring it up in divorce or family court proceedings. It is the best time to air any concerns like this, as it allows for legally binding documentation of these concerns and unique arrangements.

It is unnecessary to all, but horror stories about people who have tried to "play nice" with the narcissist didn't end well for them. The basic rule of thumb is always skeptical of a narcissist's motives, especially when your children are involved.

With children, things are always more complicated. That's just the nature of things. Even if your narcissistic ex isn't dangerous or particularly toxic to the child, their personality requires some explanation level.

Your child also needs to learn to heal and come to grips to realize that one of their parents is a narcissist. Children of narcissists often need to have it explained that the situation is not their fault.

They probably need to have their self-esteem rebuilt. They may need to learn a variety of tactics that allow them to deal with their narcissistic parents that don't cause the child undue hardship.

Whether you have children or not, rebuilding your life after being with a narcissist is not something that happens overnight.

It takes time, self-care, and a lot of reflection.

You need a strong support network that can be the shoulder you need to cry on and your rock in times of need. Your friends and family want to be this for you; all you have to do is let them. Your relationship with the narcissist may have alienated you from much of your social circle. Still, perhaps the best freedom after this kind of relationship is taking back the control over your life and rebuilding that circle stronger than before.

It is not something that happens overnight. Being with your narcissist ex can be a traumatizing experience. If you are a child by a narcissist, you may spend much of your adult life trying to come to terms with and get over your venture. Be patient and give yourself time.

There is no set rubric on how to heal or a specified time frame on how long it should take you to "get over it." Anyone trying to push you along in your efforts to heal is doing a disservice to your needs.

Many people find solace in throwing themselves into their work, hobbies, or finding a cause they can get involved with. Especially right after the breakup, you don't want to be left with your feelings as it is natural to start to look back, nostalgically, and forget why you left to begin with, especially if you are lonely.

Don't get yourself lonely or become preoccupied with the breakup. If you stay busy and don't wallow in the past, you will help yourself rebuild your life.

Put yourself on a pedestal for a change. Being with your narcissist ex means that your sense of self has taken a backseat to your partners. Once you have escaped, one of the most liberating things you can do to rebuild yourself stronger than before is to put yourself first for a change.

Focus on what you want, your feelings, your desires, your wishes. Look for ways to better care for yourself and ensure that you never let someone else take this away from you again.

Love can blind people to certain realities. It means we will often overlook red flags or things that should be obvious warning signs. People who attempt to leave a narcissist often find that if they don't cut off all contact, their narcissistic partner can coerce them into coming back through a wide range of means, we described above.

They use common tactics such as guilt-tripping, promising change, and even showering you with gifts to get you back in their proverbial clutches.

Your leaving them is a direct threat to their ability to control the world around them, leading them to act out against you in aggressive ways.

There are no short stories about the horrors of trying to divorce a narcissist. They will drag their feet through the proverbial mud; they will try to rewrite history, they will try to take you for everything you have if for no other reason than that you had the nerve to leave them.

Remaking your life after divorcing your narcissist ex is a struggle and something that you should not rush or try to do independently. The narcissist often breaks down their victims to the point that they are a shell of their former self. They have withdrawn, lost all self-esteem, no longer have an outside support network, and finally get the strength to leave; they are lost in the world. It is natural, but this doesn't mean that you should stay with the narcissist.

1) Why Are Narcissists So Attractive?

Many people feel as if narcissists are drawn to them like magnets. It may not be that narcissists are more drawn to you, but you may be more at holding on to them. For instance, many people who can easily see the negative attributes such as their need to be the center of attention, the constant reassurance they are seeking, or the sensitivity they have to be slighted. When they see these things, they may not recognize them as narcissistic traits, but they are still unfavorable. Because these are unfavorable traits, most people will not go any further with the relationship.

People are often disturbed by the types of behaviors that the narcissist displays. They will disengage from the situation because it is easier than trying to deal with someone difficult from the very beginning. The people that tend to stick around the Narcissist will handle this type of situation in a very different way.

Exiting a relationship because you feel that someone is taking advantage of you or having nefarious intent is not wrong. It may seem challenging to weed out the narcissists, but you are merely giving them more time to manipulate and take advantage of you when you give people too many chances.

All of these traits fall into the desires of a narcissist. They will do all means to take advantage of your kindness, compassion, and empathy. Most people don't try and hide these positive attributes that they hold. Unfortunately, with this, the Narcissist can pick their target quite easily.

Narcissists also genuinely enjoy taking advantage of knowledgeable people. Everything in their lives is a game, and roping someone into their smart game feels like a significant win for the Narcissist. The high they get from besting an intelligent person is better than many others.

It's unfortunate because many intelligent people end up being taken advantage of without realizing what is going on before it is way too late. They have suffered trauma at the hands of the Narcissist for far too long.

Why Are You So Attracted to Narcissists?

If it's true that narcissists are living in constant existential terror, why are people so attracted to them?

Narcissists can be very good at exploiting other people's desires to feel consequential and special. Narcissists who are high in antisocial traits—being deceptive, manipulative, hostile, or lacking empathy or remorse—may do this intentionally. Still, much of the time, it is not something done with malicious intent. Instead, it is a by-product of the Narcissist's cycles of idealization and devaluation. Think back to the metaphor of the floor built over the bottomless pit. The Narcissist wants to feel like the floor is entirely constructed and can never collapse. What better way to feel perfectly safe than to ask someone with excellent credentials to come over and inspect it? In this example, you're the inspector with excellent credentials. The Narcissist idealizes you at first, thereby giving you the authority to make him or her feel safe and reassured. In effect, you are being used by the Narcissist in the same way that a young child might use a parent for reassurance. Gradually, cracks begin to appear in the Narcissist's idealization of you. He begins to realize that you are not a perfect being. It makes the Narcissist feel insecure like maybe the floor could collapse. The Narcissist feels betrayed by your failure to remain perfect. He may even become angry with you and start to criticize you for any little imperfection. The Narcissist is projecting his insecurities onto you, filling you up with his bad feelings. You were once perfect, but now you are no good. The Narcissist must distance himself from you to avoid feeling like the floor will collapse.

As this process unfolds, you start to become desperate to regain the good feelings you associate with being idealized. You become caught in the Narcissist's gravity. The Narcissist gazes longingly at the mirror, while you gaze longingly at the Narcissist.

Now that we have a prior understanding of the Narcissist characteristics and how he/she interacts socially on a broad scale, let's take a close look at how a relationship unfolds between a narcissist and an unsuspecting victim. One of the first things victims in his situation might pick up on is that the Narcissist will be careless about consistency and repetitiveness because they do not care what others think or feel. When she confronts him about this behavior, he will easily deny it and tell her she is making things up—another gaslight symptom. It depends on the victim how far this will go. Some people have strung along for years and years. Eventually, the Narcissist will disappear and then reappear sporadically. They tell his victim that he is unsure about things and feels insecure about their relationship, perhaps pointing out something that the victim has done wrong in the relationship that makes him doubt her commitment, etc. The Narcissist will use anything and everything to inflict pain and make the victim feel like they need to make up for something they've done.

Eventually, the game is going to end, one way or another. The Narcissist will often not let go for a very long time, even if they are leaving for long periods in between their reappearances. Depending on how strong their chains have become connected to their victims, the victims will wait and hope and pray until the future time they see their narcissist partners. The emotional pain and control have run so deep that they do not feel they can live any other way.

When we think of women in physically abusive relationships, many people find it too easy to pass judgment on them, suggesting that she needs to leave. The fact is until you've experienced the kind of emotional abuse and manipulation exercised by an abusive partner, it is impossible to understand just how much a person can twist another human being's reality. Abuse victims often cite how they slipped into a state of denial or were so convinced that they were the problem in the relationship that they tolerated the abuse and blamed themselves for it happening. It is a sad but true reality. Don't ever pass judgment on an abuse victim until you know what you're talking about. And even then, we must all realize that each of us is unique and that we all have different constitutions, strengths, and weaknesses. How many times have you heard it from someone that they never thought they'd be dumb enough to fall for that, etc.

It's important not to internalize a feeling of being "dumb" if you've fallen victim to narcissistic abuse. The fact is that these people do nothing with their lives except getting better and better at manipulating and hurting others. They are professionals, and they are experts. You are not an idiot for being human and having feelings. You have run into someone who knows exactly how to take advantage of your common human decency and kindness.

Many victims have strung along for the rest of their lives to die in misery and isolation without ever having received what they needed and wanted from a romantic partner. A victim goes through emotionally throughout a narcissist abuse experience is harrowing, and the effects are long-lasting.

2) Having A Relationship with A Narcissist

A narcissistic relationship differs significantly from a relationship with an average person. Even the love and attention they will shower on you at the onset is way too much. Any sensitive person would smell a rat, but humans, wired to crave love, will gravitate toward the best feeling provided by another.

Here are the pointers that show you are in a relationship with a narcissist:

You Always Feel Bad About Yourself

A relationship should make you happy, feel worthy, and feel loved. A relationship with narcissists is characterized by various manipulation and mind games, gaslighting, criticizing, and devaluation. They use many tactics to make you question your judgment and sanity. The abuse can get so critical that you feel you don't know yourself again. It is typical of a narcissistic relationship. It is also common for partners to:

- Feel like everything they do annoys the narcissist
- Become separated from friends and loved ones

- Constantly question themselves
- Think all they do is wrong

Feeling inadequate in a relationship could be caused by what the other person said or did. At times, they might not even say or do anything. It could be their reaction.

They might shun you; roll their eyes at you when you say something etc. When you try to question their attitude; they will tell you are too sensitive.

They Are Mainly Interested in Talking About Themselves

The ideal conversation is usually two-ways, and it occurs naturally. It is not the same as a narcissist. They tend to dominate the conversation and direct it towards themselves. If you attempt to change the subject, they will interrupt. If you notice that your partner is hardly interested in talking about you and things that interest you, you might be in a narcissist relationship. Due to their tendency to always be in charge, they control the conversation as well. Hence, they are either doing all the talking or not responding to you at all. Either way, they are in control.

An Alarming Sense of Entitlement

As opposed to a healthy and normal relationship that is symbiotic and reciprocal, a narcissistic relationship is not. The narcissist will act as if they deserve something, anything from you, rather than working for it. You will see them shy away from their responsibility for you or another person to do it. If you are in a relationship and your partner refuses to get a job despite the tight financial situation, he might be a narcissist.

If they are not getting enough money, support, care, you will see them display eccentric behavior to get what they want. It can be likened to the three-year-old tantrum throws to get attention.

They Are Initially Charming

It is so, so easy to miss the qualities of a narcissistic partner at first. It is not surprising as that was how they were able to get you entangled in their web. No one in their right senses will fall for all the mind games of a narcissist. As a result, they come at you disguised with many charming qualities that you will find irresistible.

In time, you will see their true nature. If it suddenly feels like all the love your partner has for you died and transformed into a cold and mean stranger, you'll know.

They Hardly Compromise

Remember that a narcissist lives in a fantasy world where everything should pan out as they have it in their head. They so much believe in their views that every other person's opinion does not matter. They will neither try to understand your point, let alone consider it.

It is healthy for two parties in a relationship to disagree at times and have varying opinions. However, if your partner is not interested in your perspective, he is likely a narcissist.

Stages of a Narcissistic Relationship

The main reason for getting into a relationship is to connect, love, and share with another person. A narcissist's reason for getting into a relationship differs significantly. They are incapable of love, so the typical romantic bond is not possible.

More than any other person, narcissists need people. They need people to keep their sense of being, self-worth, and self-esteem up. This void is present in the narcissists that can only be filled by others' love and admiration. It is what they care about. It is what prompts them to enter a relationship. They are not after watching for you or sharing your joy and pain. When they see anyone that can be a source for them, they will go to any means to make this person fall for them, even if it means putting up a false perception.

The relationship with a narcissist follows four phases:

- The love-bombing stage
- The devaluation stages
- The discarding stage
- The return

We will inspect each of these in detail throughout this guide.

Love-Bombing Stage

One of the motivations of a narcissist in choosing a partner is what they can get from them. That is why they often go after rich people, people with class and influence, people with attractive bodies, etc.

Once they have their target, a narcissist directs all their effort and energy in chasing the victim. They are so meticulous in their pursuit that they project the image the victim craves for. It is like a little boy that becomes infatuated with a shiny new tricycle. He pesters his parents so much they have no choice but to get him the tricycle. On getting the tricycle, this boy rides it every day and any spare moment he has is on the toy. He goes everywhere with the tricycle. After a couple of weeks, he is fed up and wants a new toy. They will bombard their target with so much love; it seems they idolize them. The narcissists will share all their hopes and dreams with you freely and seem interested in yours. Unfortunately, however, the victim often gets carried away to get so convinced they have found a life-partner. Remember, what the narcissists does majorly is mirror what they know appeals to their target. It convinces the target without a doubt that this person is for them.

The Devaluation Stage

For most narcissists, the love-bombing stage lasts between a couple of weeks to a few months. All they need is sufficient time to be sure you are already entangled in their web, you are head over heels in love and committed to them. Unfortunately, many targets are clueless because all they are seeing is the narcissist with a mask of what appeals to them. It is the phase where they show their true colors.

This stage begins slowly and subtly at first. Their commitment, faithfulness will die down. They become moody, stop returning your calls, getting irritated quickly at what you say or do. You get confused, thinking it is something you said or did. They were supposed to be in love with you; why would they treat you this bad? The reason is to have total control over you. Narcissist's aim of mistreating their victim is to gradually destroy themselves in yourself and others, your self-worth, and self-esteem. Their behavior and attitude get so cruel that it leaves you bewildered. A partner should be supportive and loving, but suddenly it seems like a switch flipped, and they transformed. Nothing you do is ever appreciated, and they even call you as clingy if you try to maintain the usual amount of commitment and passion that you once shared.

Narcissists tend to get bored with people quickly, which usually starts in their heads. They start telling themselves there was nothing special about you after all. The slightest provocation will set them off, and they will lash out at you firmly. They are never present, and even when they are, their minds are miles away. As the narcissist withdraws, the partner, in a bid to keep the fire burning, clings in demand for his attention. However, all your clinging only drives him further away and even gets him angry. Their target takes the blame and criticism for everything that goes wrong.

It often wrecks the partner emotionally. What could have happened to their supposed "soul mate?" What many victims do not realize is that the veil is just falling off. It is the person behind the cover that they are just meeting. However, they try desperately to find the person they fell in love with, with no avail. Unknown to them, this person never existed. They were only victims of the narcissist manipulation to secure their supply.

Any ill-treatment the narcissist caused you don't bother them. They were never capable of forming healthy bonding in the first place. All you experienced was a facade.

At this stage, they have succeeded in making you scramble for their love. This way, you try with all you might to please them and succumb to their demands, with the hope that the person you fell in love with comes back. They might resort to criticizing everything about you. It could be your friends and loved ones. They will make you uncomfortable in front of your family and loved ones, so you begin to avoid them. Not only that, but they will also always find fault in your appearance. As long as it does not appeal to them, as long as it makes you outshine them, they will criticize and condemn it.

Either of two things will happen; Your narcissist partner might have found a new target and directed all their attention on them, making them ignore you. Or you decide you are done with the games and end it, bringing in the third phase.

The Discard Stage

To the narcissist, you are only a pawn. You are only relevant to the narcissist because they used you to fulfill a need. As soon as the demand is fulfilled, they will discard you faster than an old newspaper. The ease with which a narcissist pulls away from their partner once their usefulness is exhausted is alarming. Many people will ask themselves over and over:

- Did I mean anything to him?
- Did he even care about me?

The brutal answer is, No. the narcissists are not capable of love and emotions. You were just a source of power for them. You were only relevant as long as they could feed off of you. Once they have had enough of you, you will be shoved off the pedestal without mercy and warning.

Any attempt to oppose them will be met with strict resistance, and if you are dealing with a brutal one, they can go as far as destroying you. Remember, you never meant anything to them, so they will not think twice before leaving. They only care about a single individual in the entire world, which is themselves.

The Return

If you manage to get this stage of a narcissistic relationship, you are free. By this time, the narcissist is out of your house. Even though it is hard and challenging at first, you will improve. The storm is over, and your life will be calmer and smoother with less stress. It is the stage where you need to start looking after yourself. All the energy you directed at supporting and caring for your ex should be directed at taking care of yourself.

3) Getting Married to a Narcissist

You may have a narcissist among your family; you may enter a workplace with a narcissistic person; there may be one among your acquaintances, or you may fall for a narcissistic person. Unfortunately, there are many ways in which you can encounter. But, what happens when you fall and get married to a narcissistic?

The narcissists are always on the lookout for new "supply," i.e., people who will give them attention, no matter if that attention is positive or negative. A narcissistic person feels alive when interacting with others. In external relations, they can mirror all the deliciousness they see in others, as something they hold themselves.

For instance, narcissistic persons always fall for people who contain whichever qualities they want themselves. They will create an alliance with you; making you believe that they hold precisely the same attributes as you do, or that their qualities fit perfectly with yours. In other words: The narcissist will mirror himself in you so you feel important and unique.

The narcissist might say things like: "You are so unique. Your sensitivity and your huge compassion for others make you extra vulnerable. I am just the same, and people like us must take care of one another." Or: "You are so strong and so much in control of your life. It is rare to meet a kindred spirit, who is as wise as you are."

Observe that these statements emphasize the two of you as someone who both possess the same characteristics, and therefore you have something special in common. Of course, the narcissist keeps them — otherwise, he or he couldn't recognize them within you — but they are not activated. They will never show in daily life, which you will find after being together on Cloud Nine, after getting married to him. The characteristics are hidden beneath extremely low self-worth, and they are rarely in use — only to gain power or other advantages in the relationship with others.

The narcissist dreams of the one true love, and he is truly capable of putting on a show and "love bomb" you with words, caresses, adventures, money, gifts, sex, or whatever the narcissist senses that you need to lure you into their spider's web.

You will feel that no one has ever loved you so intensely or truly before. You have never been seen and understood so beautifully and sensibly, as the narcissist does. That is hard to resist, and if you are deceived and caught in his web, it doesn't mean that you are less intelligent or naïve than others. We all want to feel loved, feel unique and essential, and what the narcissist gives you. For a short while — and that is the problem. It is nothing but hot air, and it doesn't last.

The narcissist will be busy trying to commit you with children, money, duties, essential job functions, marriage, buying a house, or anything else, making it hard for you to turn your back on him and walk away.

All relationships, or most of them, begin in the seventh heaven as something special, until your married life forms, the gilt cracks and reveals that this is not just a fixer-upper, but an unfixable ruin of a human being, who accept neither sense nor sensibility. However, in the beginning, you will become the prince or princess, the center of all fairytales. It doesn't last. Over and over, you will experience the cycle with which the narcissist slowly destroys you. It is on infinite repeat.

Love bombing begins with idealization. Then follows devaluation, and then rejection. At first, you will be regarded as the most fantastic creature which the universe has ever encountered. Then, you will be torn to pieces and humiliated, and lastly, you will be rejected and deemed useless.

Since you don't understand that this is an unhealthy pattern, it may be difficult to see through it, and that's why you will react like everybody else: You will try fixing it. You will take responsibility, and your thoughts will run in circles, trying to find a solution.

You will do everything in your power to make him happy - and you will fail. "If I just do this and that, then we will find our way back to love and the unique essence of our relationship," – and this attitude gives the narcissist precisely what he wants: attention and power. The cycle will repeat itself, and the "love," which you long for, becomes a lesser and lesser part of your relationship. At the same time, the devaluation of you grows, until you are convinced that you are the one, who broke and trashed the love, and that you are a terrible and unlovable person.

However, it doesn't mean that you shall keep from falling in love, or that you have to be on guard toward people who see and value your good qualities.

What you must do is have a strong relationship with yourself, thus enabling you to feel that you are "enough" without another person's acceptance, approval, or need for you. Then you are free to walk away as soon as it becomes unpleasant, and your boundaries are disrespected. You will become more challenging to manipulate and brainwashed into believing that you owe someone something or that you must live up to certain expectations.

Ask yourself: "If I wasn't trying to fix things and make him happy all the time, would he want me?" If the answer is no, you are merely a facilitator, and your relationship is fake, challenging as it is to realize.

Why do you think that you were the one falling for the superficial charm of the narcissist and got poorly treated?

"Because I am too quiet? No. Because I take up too much space? No. Because I am a terrible human being? No. Because I am stupid? No. Because I am annoying? No. Because I deserved it? No. Because I provoked him? No. Because I am easily fooled? No. Because I don't function with others? No. Because I allowed it? No. Because I am a loser? No. Because I attracted it? No. Because I am too naïve? No. Because I am different from others? No. Because I am a pleaser? No. Because I believed the lies? No.

Because I am too delicate? No. Because I was also open? No. Because I was too trusting? No. Because I ignored the warning signals? No. Because a narcissist abuses and misuses others? Yes.

Getting married to a narcissist, the relationship you'll build with him will be unhealthy, especially when you have children around, and you should think about what you want to do going forward. Do you want to spend the upcoming 10 or 20 or even 30 years trying to please somebody who will never be happy?

Do you want to spend the rest of your life with someone who does not care about your feelings in any way? That's no way to live.

4) Why Is A Narcissist Getting Married?

In terms of marriage, a narcissist's games and deceptions do not make for the best partner. There is no partnership present at all, perhaps only in fleeting moments. Partnership implies unity, harmony, and mutual respect, trust, and connection. All a narcissist has to offer is mind games, suffering, confusion, and oppression. It can be highly oppressive living and being with a narcissist as they don't like to see you happy, thriving, or succeeding in your own goals, dreams, and aspirations.

Before going into the eight reasons why a narcissist gets married, let's first discover five things to watch out for.

The Need to Control

Narcissists are overly controlling. They see their partner as a target or supply for their deep-seated manipulations and need to control. Fortunately, you can spot this tendency early on, creating better boundaries and inner strength. It can be more difficult once you are already enticed and wrapped around their little finger, but if you can remain strong and centered from the start, then there shouldn't be a problem with recognizing this sign that you are with a narcissist.

This control reflects in many areas. It may be your clothes, beliefs, daily habits, actions, likes and dislikes, and holistic identity and sense of self. Whichever the expression, you cannot be you or be free to make your own life choices.

Emotion- Phobia

Narcissists are terrified of emotions. It is not about manipulation or using malicious and harmful emotional intents to cause pain or chaos, but it is talking about real and sincere feelings and connections. Unlike in normal relationships where love, care, and affection are prevalent, narcissists are incapable of real intimacy and subsequently see marriage as a way to exert their dominance and emotional superiority. Of course, the narcissist is not in any way, shape, or form emotionally superior- however, they see themselves as better than you somehow. It is because of the distorted view that emotions and vulnerability are weak and inferior.

A Fragmented Family History

There will always be some aspect of childhood trauma, repressions, and family stories with your narcissistic partner. Most people see childhood or family-related wounds as a way to self- develop, heal, and transcend wounds and pains brought from childhood. Yet a narcissist is so afraid of vulnerability and looking to the core of themselves that the patterns and wounds brought from childhood will show their ugly face in your relationship. Your partner will use projection as a means to hide from their issues, also masking their inner securities and wounds with harmful and hurtful displays, words, and behaviors.

Projection: You as Their Mirror

You are essentially their mirror. Like projecting their family traumas and childhood wounds, the narcissists perceive you as their mirror or shield to their ignorance. Many things require patience, understanding, and compassion; a desire to help and heal one another is instead met with projection. Imagine throwing a ball at a wall. Regardless of how many times the ball hits the wall, it will always bounce back. The ball is symbolic of the narcissist's intentions, motivation, and inner turmoil, and the wall is you. You are their shield and structure to bounce off and keep their games in play. Regardless of the negative trait, situation, story, or destructive intention, the narcissist will always see you as someone to stand by their side or in front of them to take their 'stuff.'

Insecurities Masked as Arrogance

You will know you are with a narcissist when their deeply buried insecurities start to come to light. They will always be masked as arrogance, a false sense of superiority, self- centeredness, an inflated ego, and other less desirable personality traits. Real displays of vulnerability, raw emotion, and soft feelings or moods, which are natural and a part of our humanity, will never be shown. Wounds, traumas, doubts, fears, and general self- discovery or self- development are all covered by a need to appear the best, all together, omniscient, and forcefully superior. There is no sense of room and space for healing, and in the narcissist's eye, they are already perfect. They want you to believe they are excellent too, and anything which threatens their sense of self- created status is met with abuse, manipulation, or projection- like tactics.

8 Reason Why a Narcissist Gets Married

It brings us to why a narcissist gets married. Hopefully, this will prevent a future marriage or relationship with a narcissist.

A Scapegoat

Unfortunately, you are their scapegoat. Like in the signs and things to watch out for, a narcissist sees you as their mirror to project all their stuff. You will be condemned for all of their wrongdoings, judged and persecuted for the narcissist's mistake, faults, and negative traits. It is how narcissists fundamentally view marriage; they see their partner as a tool for shifting blame and passing responsibility. The sad truth is that they need this, hence why they choose to get married.

To Perpetuate Their Insecurities/ Traumas/ Emotional Wounds

One reason why a narcissist gets married is to perpetuate their insecurities, traumas, and wounds. Remember that narcissists have some deep vulnerabilities which they are too afraid to admit. Narcissists can live their whole lives in states of inner depression, chaos, and turmoil, and with further repressions and unresolved wounds and pains; without ever healing or transcending from them. Their narcissism is simply a cover and a shield to hide them from their wounds. Like with anything in life, we are social and family-oriented creatures. It means that they need someone to bounce off, be with a support system, and mirror. Unfortunately, you will be their rock and gem in a method that drains you, depletes you, and leaves you feeling psychologically and mentally abused.

To Keep Their Illusions Intact

They need you to stay fooled and enticed in their games and manipulations. The saying there is "support or power in numbers" applies here. In marriage, the narcissist receives your love and support, which empowers them and keeps their narcissistic ways in the sense of acceptance. Something cannot exist without energy, awareness, and thumbs up from people. It is we human beings who create and shape reality as we know it. It is one of the key reasons why a narcissist gets married because they know that their illusions will only survive and thrive through another's support. Again, you become like their rock or gem. This support may be unconscious or based on you being fooled and stuck in their games; however, it is still a green light.

For Peers and Colleagues

What better way to keep one's social illusions of charm and eloquence in play then to have a level- headed, regular and sincere partner on their arm? Having a wife is the foundation that keeps their self- created identity at play. The narcissist appears normal and even kind, wise, and beautiful to peers and colleagues when they have a sane partner by their side. Yet, it is not reciprocated and leaves you clinging onto the idea and false reality that your partner is charming and is capable of real social grace, kindness, and companionship. When you are alone again, you will once again be the target of their games and abuse.

Self-Identity and Appearance

They need a partner for their success, self- identity, and appearance. Your love and sanity fuel their professional and personal life. Companionship and intimacy are a natural and fundamental part of life, and the narcissist knows this- even if they can't display real intimacy and companionship themselves. They hide behind you and your favorable beautiful qualities, always making them appear in a positive light. Their self- identity and public or professional/ personal persona depend on this. If you were to withdraw your support, who would they be? They could be exposed in their real character, or their hidden intentions and motivations could be brought to the surface. Marriage to a sane, sincere, and non- narcissistic partner is the perfect shield.

The Charm Illusion

Most people would not choose a partner or lifelong companion if they knew they would be psychologically and emotionally abusive, manipulative, and holistically speaking, lacking in such empathy. So, this is the precise reason why a narcissist needs a marriage partner. Who would want to be married to a narcissist and enter such a formal and long-standing agreement? The answer is no one- no one would willingly or consciously choose this. It all, therefore, comes down to the charm illusion, the illusion from the start of your connection that your partner is charming, decent, and sincere. If their husbands or wives see them as beautiful, kind, and worthy of a loving and supportive marriage, why wouldn't others see them as excellent in other aspects of life? A narcissist depends on friends, peers, and colleagues' support and love, so having yours is the first and primary step. You are like the anchor, cement, and seed all in one. Without you, the narcissist is nothing. "The charm illusion" is essentially the delusions and harmful stories your partner can keep through your acceptance and compassionate, yet self-detrimental, support.

To Be in Control

Like with the things to watch out for, a narcissist needs to be in control. In other words, they need someone to control. It may be a hard truth to accept, but you are ultimately their plaything. Without someone to handle, command, or order, the narcissist's illusions begin to break down. Without their fantasies, their world falls apart, so they need this false sense of superiority and dominance. If you are not cooperative and present in their games and intentions, how would they maintain their illusion of control, or 'having it all together?' The truth is that the narcissist is not all together, in any way, shape, or form. It is their marriage partner's compliance that allows it.

To Never Have to Heal

One of the primary and arguably most significant reasons why a narcissist gets married is that they never have to heal when they have someone to bounce off and project all their own 'stuff' onto. You are their scapegoat, mirror, shield, rock, gem, projection wall, and foundation all in one! Any unresolved traumas represent wounds, past pains, sadistic and narcissistic traits, characteristics, and personal issues that become accepted and integrated once a narcissist enters the marriage. Most people do the work before entering into a partnership as they realize that they should be the best version of themselves before committing to someone. Many people don't want to project their unresolved things in companionship. For this reason alone, the idea of never having to heal or better themselves for both their partner and them self is unspeakable. Healing and self- development are a natural part of life.

However, the narcissist marriage is a means of escape. They can escape from their past, their wounds, their narcissism, and their often 'evil' and sadistic intentions; through the presence and cover of a life partner. They are incapable of having a healthy, intimate, and cooperative or supportive relationship, and the lack of empathy and compassion is too prevalent to overlook. Even if you are strong beyond belief, you will still be the sufferer in the marriage due to the narcissist's ability to repeatedly break your heart.

5) Narcissist Betrayals

Narcissism in a relationship is very demanding. A narcissistic partner whose traits have fully developed cannot change no matter what you do. This stage can be without even the narcissistic partner knowing about it. He receives excitement each time he makes the partner feel bad. He enjoys the tears and because they make him feel more substantial and superior. When a partner complains about him, it is like fueling the desires. A fully developed narcissistic partner will show the following betrayals:

Dishonesty in Healthy Relationships

Factors like harassment, fear, stress, anxiety, and other emotional disturbances can cause deception. A narcissist's case is different. He will cheat in the relationship because it is in his nature. He wants his desires fulfilled. He might not be finding the one thing he thinks will satisfy him. Therefore, he will cheat to go out and like for that thing. Narcissists will always lie when in relationships. They will shift words or say something that does not exist so that they can gain attention. When they lie, they get the admiration of others, and this is an achievement to them. Their sense of excessive appreciation will be fulfilled.

Narcissistic partners will promise things that they will not fulfill to get the praises. They do this without caring about the feelings of the partner when they do not deliver upon promises. They live in the current situation and do not think of tomorrow or the day after.

Arrogance

They will behave in a manner that makes you feel worthless. They do not care about your feelings, and if you ask them, they will either deny or answer you rudely. They will make critical decisions in the relationship without asking or involving you. They can make decisions like buying a car, withdrawing a massive amount from your joint account, filing a divorce, etc. Their arrogance can sometimes extend to the partner's guests and even friends. Since narcissist partners do not approve anything you do, they sometimes do not approve of your friends. Their arrogance will go to the extent of talking to your friends the way they like without any boundaries. They will be little your family members and answer rudely in case of any questions.

Lack of Empathy

A narcissistic partner lacks empathy. His primary focus is his desires. He wants to receive praise for delivering a particular project or draw attention by doing a sure thing. His partner cannot stop these desires because he will become very aggressive. His objectives hold the priorities. Whether they step on you or not, it does not bother them. He will make sure his desires are successful even when it means going through his partner. He has no thoughts of how the partner will feel after finding out about his deeds. When a partner is sick, he will not help. He does not car care how much pain the partner is going through. All he will focus on is his needs. If he wants to eat and the partner is sick, they cannot cook. He will complain about the laziness of the partner. He will call the partner names. A narcissistic partner can never feel his partner's pain, whether he has caused it or not.

Are Controlling

Control in relationships is not inadequate, especially if its purpose is for the relationship's better good. For example, if a partner controls the misuse of money in the relationship, this is for the courtship's productivity. He is probably saving the money for a developmental project that will help the future. But if your partner controls everything, then you should be careful. A partner that manages how you talk, dress, eat, spend your time, the hairstyle, and so many others is a control freak. He is doing all this to feel better about himself.

He is trying to exercise his power on you to feed his superiority deficiency syndrome. He has cared for you in his mind. He sees you as a tool to satisfy his ego. He wants to make a point that he is in charge, and you are the victim. Suppose you accept everything he tells you to do in the relationship. In that case, you will be fueling him, and he will end, bringing harm to your emotional and physical health beyond imagination.

Boastful

He will boast of how he can make the problem disappear in the relations. In the end, they do not have solutions to the issues. They will boast about how progressive they are to capture the attention of the people. They will boast of how they are connected to high-status people to get exceptional care and attention.

When your partner regularly boasts about how the relationship is working because of him to get unnecessary attention. When he takes children to any good schools, he brags about it; then, you have to know that his condition is full-blown. He has reached the highest point of narcissism, and he needs dire help for him to recover.

Envious

He is a very jealous person. He does not want his partner to do anything that may bring attention. All his attention belongs to him, and he will always make sure he steals the spot. He will envy his partner's new car even when they are staying together. He will pretend to like something his partner has done only to trash back the partner. He can also tell the partner a particular thing is not good so that he can go ahead and have it.

Negative Attitude

Having a negative attitude towards everything will make people walk away from you. Nobody likes people who do not support them or their projects. A narcissist partner who has reached a full-blown stage always has a negative attitude. He will never endorse anything that the partner proposes. For example, if a partner is an excellent teacher who has several, he will negatively affect the teaching profession. The reason is that the job of his partner is stealing the spotlight away from him. He believes that he is the only person that should be praised or appreciated.

Selfish

If you are always fighting with your partner for not supporting anything you do, and all his needs are a priority, he is a developed narcissist. The only help he needs is mental help from an experienced mental health practitioner. His feelings and needs are always a priority, and he does not care if the partner has other things to do. He expects the partner to handle all his needs before attending to any different requirements.

A narcissistic partner will not reciprocate love given to them by their partners. They cannot do this because they are so selfish even to love themselves. They believe they are no one worthy of their love. They are afraid that there cannot receive the love back if they gave it out, so they keep it to themselves. They are selfish that they do not keep in mind the feelings of their partners before doing anything. There aims for their self-importance. They are s blinded by selfishness that they cannot know the best things in the relationship.

Passive Self-importance

His need for self-importance is less obvious, and if you are not keen, you might realize it. You will only feel the weariness and tiredness of the behaviors after some time. The covert narcissistic partner excessively wants attention and admiration, but he will make you feel different.

He will give back all the praises you give him and pretend to love you again. He will delay completing projects so that you acknowledge how important he is in the project. He loves hearing you say how his importance unmeasurable. A covert narcissistic partner has a delicate sense of self, which is why he wants you to see him as remarkable.

Blaming and Shaming

He will gently explain how the things that went wrong are your fault, and he is not the one to blame. He will make you feel like it is all your fault until you start blaming yourself.

You will feel sorry for him that he had to go through the problems you caused. He wants to get the praises from you. He is trying to tell you that you are worthless. You do not match his standards, and without him, you cannot make it. Generally, he wants you to be ashamed and never try and do anything or oppose what he said.

Creation of Confusion

They will make you start doubting your decisions; they will brainwash you into wanting to change your perceptions. You will feel that you have been wrong, so you need to change. All these deeds from them make them feel superior. They want you to praise them for helping, and they will feel significant.

They will create confusion to make you weak so that they can exploit you the way they want. Covert narcissistic partners will make you feel like they help you get decisions or solutions to your problems. But in the real sense, they are confusing. They know that when you are confused, you cannot make decisions at all, and you will see them as necessary when they come up with the solutions.

Disregard

They are not afraid of proving you are worthless, but their approach is different and confusing. For example, if a covert narcissistic partner arranged for a date with you, he will stand you up or come very late without communicating. He will not give you a reason as to why he did not go or why he came late.

He does not provide any regard to the relationship, for your interests and your time. He feels he is the worthier person and can do whatever he wants at any time. He is a professional at disregarding you. He makes you have so many thoughts, and you might even end up convincing yourself that maybe he was held up in something else that he did not make it to the date.

Emotionally Neglectful

They may seem kind to you and less rude, but they are emotionally inaccessible. The covert narcissistic partner will not compliment you on anything for they feel so elevated, and their self-importance matters more. He will not appreciate your abilities or talents. He cannot reciprocate the love and care you give him. You will find yourself in the relationship handling all the emotional issues while your covert narcissistic partner does not care. However, they will appear emotionally attached to you and accessible only when he has a motive of exploiting you or making you feel ashamed or small.

6) The Violence/Cruelty of a Narcissist in Marriage

Violence and cruelty when you marry a narcissist is a widespread thing. Different kind of abuse happens in a relationship with a narcissistic partner listed below are some of them:

Domestic Abuse/Violence
Domestic abuse occurs when your narcissist spouse tries to dominate and control you. He has only one purpose: to gain and maintain control over the other party. He uses the weapons of fear, guilt, shame, and intimidation to manipulate his victim into submission. When physical violence is involved, it becomes known as domestic violence.
It occurs regardless of age, race, or economic status. The forms may include coercion, threats, isolation, and emotional, sexual, and physical abuse against the other spouse or other persons associated with her.
An abuser tends to exert power and control over his partner. It is generally believed that domestic violence results from anger, but it is not always so. It is about instilling fear and a desire to demonstrate power and control over other(s) in a relationship.

A batterer may also resort to physical violence such as kicking, shoving, slapping, etc. He may also use sexual violence, such as forcing his partner to have sexual intercourse with him against her will or consent. Domestic violence usually starts subtly. In an abusive relationship, several tactics deployed by an abuser to gain power and control over the other include:

Economic Abuse
The narcissist exercises total and absolute control over the finances and refuse to share money or may not allow you to work outside the home. It is to ensure total dependence on him by the abused mate.

Emotional Abuse
The narcissist uses insults and criticisms to make you feel bad about himself.
Intimidation: It involves using detailed looks, actions, and gestures to frighten and instill fear in the other person.
Isolation: It involves limiting contacts with friends and family, not allowing you to go to work, controlling your social activities, tracking your time and whereabouts, etc.
Power: The narcissist makes all the significant decisions in the relationship, is in charge of domestic and social life, and treats the partner like a servant or possession. This abuse is common, especially in Africa, where the cultural concept enforces it.
Criticism: The narcissist may start with criticizing the appearance of the other or maybe unreasonably jealous. Gradually this becomes frequent and may eventually assume a life-threatening dimension. Major characteristics of a life-threatening violent relationship include the following:
Hitting, kicking, shoving, or being threatened with violence; having no choice about how to spend one's time, where to go or what to wear; being falsely accused of what one did or did not do; having to ask the narcissist partner for permission to make everyday decisions; submitting to sex or engaging in ungodly or dehumanizing sexual acts against one's will; accepting the narcissist decisions out of fear of ensuing anger, and accused of being unfaithful.

Spousal Sexual Abuse
One of the major problems in marriage, but the least addressed, which creates discord in many marriages worldwide, is the sexual abuse of a wife by her husband, also known as spousal sexual abuse or marital rape. Spousal

sexual abuse is generally defined as forcing undesired sexual acts by a marriage partner on another. Marriage is the context of this book refers to a man and his wife, who are lawfully wedded.

It is a non-consensual, forced physical, sexual behavior occurring in a marriage. It is domestic violence where sexual abuses are perpetrated by one spouse on another, usually the wife. The wife is always the primary victim of spousal sexual abuse.

Spousal sexual abuse or exploitation against the wife is a crime or atrocity that many husbands commit willfully and get away with because marriage immunes them. It naturally occurs because many religions, cultures, and laws in many parts of the world seem to recognize the 'right' or 'authority' of a husband to abuse his wife, regarded as unchallengeable sexually. The affected wives are unable to talk because there is no channel to seek redress. Therefore, they suffer in silence.

Spousal rape occurs when a husband has his way, sexually, without his wife's consent or obtains her consent under duress and pressure. The support given under pressure would be no consent if it were issued against her will. Her consent could be against her will, where she was not inclined to have sex but accepted as a duty or as a routine to avoid trouble.

Women who have sexually abused by their husbands bear the hurt silently for the following reasons:

- Societal pressures and associated social stigma
- Causes of endangering family loyalty
- Fear of their husband's possible retaliation
- Hesitation to strain the relationship
- To avoid the embarrassment, it may bring to the nuclear and the extended family.
- Many women do not accept that forced sex within marriage is equal to rape.
- Some women believe that rape occurs only when a stranger is involved.

These women see sex within marriage as a duty that must be performed even against their will and consent. Further, many victims cannot react because they are financially dependent on their husbands and cannot risk quitting the marriage because of resisting forced sex. Lastly, no one would believe them. Yet many marital relationships have silently been destroyed by this evil.

Traditional beliefs exist which say that a woman exists to please her husband sexually, whether convenient or not, and regardless of whether or not she derives pleasure from it. The belief is that the exchange of marriage vows has denied the spouse the right to say 'no' to sex. That marriage means automatic and perpetual consent to sex with the husband anytime he wants it regardless of circumstance.

This problem is mostly caused by a lack of understanding, impatience, and intolerance of the narcissist husband's part, the primary culprit.

7) Stuck In A Relationship With A Narcissist   (Reasons with Remedies)

As much as you might have heard or read about narcissists, you are not wrong to build a relationship with one. You also need to know that you are not deliberately setting yourself on the path of self-destruction. Narcissists are quite romantic and can be charming. They are great lovers and can be friends. The truth is they can be sensitive to how you feel and adjust to your needs.

However, narcissists can be very manipulative. They are complicated people; therefore, being in any relationship, whether romantic or not, spiritual or professional, you need to know that it can be confusing and be set for the situation. Narcissists are complicated and hard to understand because sometimes you will find them very helpful and dependable to point, they will seem to care about you. The truth is their devotion and kindness are mostly to benefit themselves and further put them in control of things.

Forming a relationship with a narcissist is not uncommon. Many people are in such a narcissistic relationship without even realizing it until they are far into it. A victim doesn't feel like leaving because her life is centered on the narcissist. It isn't easy to let go of such a relationship, especially if they are married and have kids. Also, at times, dealing with an ex who is a narcissist can be quite tricky.

Narcissists are potentially harmful in many ways. How do you make the relationship work? How is it possible to build a healthy relationship with a narcissist? It is indeed possible and maybe rewarding to have a relationship with someone who is a narcissist. Still, that relationship would be psychologically and emotionally draining. A narcissist usually lacks what it takes to build a healthy relationship. They do not show consistent kindness, compassion, selflessness, reciprocity, compromise, and empathy.

What to Expect if you're stuck in a Relationship with a Narcissist?

There are many challenges when we are stuck, and we can't get away to a narcissist, as we have earlier said. Still, when you are aware of some of the things to expect, you should also know how to handle the relationship better to build a healthy one.

You Will Need to Make Some Sacrifices

To have a reasonably good life or relationship with a narcissist, you need lots of sacrifices to keep the relationship going. You will sacrifice a part of you, especially your beliefs and what you stand for, and one of the expected constants is that you will be lied to repeatedly yet must accept it.

Narcissists are crafty and very manipulative. They are good at changing narratives and altering reality into the version that suits them, and in the end, they get you to agree to something that you didn't do. To keep narcissists happy, you will need to learn how to accept their version of reality as the truth of what has happened even when it is not. That way, you will always escape their fury and not be on the receiving end.

Part of the sacrifice is that you might never get praised for achieving something or rewarded for behaving well. Narcissists will, at every opportunity, try to undermine your effort. They are so manipulative to the point where they call all the shots yet in a brilliant way that will seem as though you are in control. They will let you make decisions but will do something different, and you have to appreciate them for doing that. Building healthy relationships with narcissists mean you have to play a secondary role. It would be best if you made sacrifices that will drain you in a lot of ways.

To a Narcissist, No One is to Be Trusted

Narcissists wouldn't trust anybody except themselves. Even when you do everything right and have never given them any reason not to trust you, they would still not respect you enough to allow you to lead your life without interference and surveillance. They can go to the extent of spying and stalking you.

Narcissists have the habit of tracking their partners. In a romantic relationship, narcissists are likely to install trackers without the knowledge of their partners. It could be on their phone or computer, and they feel no remorse about it but rather proud of their action.

Regrettably, most narcissists abuse drugs and alcohol to the extreme. Their partners will have to endure and adapt to their lifestyle and live with the perpetual fear and expectation that they may take things too far with the drugs or alcohol and act unpredictably.

Most narcissists usually develop bad habits and, because of that, can become so irresponsible, missing their appointments, meetings, and work. Therefore, it puts their partners in situations where they have to clean up the mess they create and make up excuses to absolve them. The reason is that the partners have been conditioned to believe that they are a team and that it's them against the whole world.

Narcissists will never put their trust in anyone; therefore, they use words that will keep their victims spellbound like "You are my world" and "Without you, I'm nothing." That way, their victims are comforted with a false sense of security. Meanwhile, they are just cutting their partners from everyone and everything, pitching them against the world and using them.

Narcissists will say things and take actions that will be convincing enough to make you believe in them. Trust them and risk it all for them. You should be ready not to be trusted when in a relationship with a narcissist.

Although it is not clear if narcissists do things intending to hurt their partners to the level they do, they excuse having a bad childhood. You must understand and forgive them for all their shortcomings and behaviors. They will explode, and you will face their rage if you don't ignore them of everything they have done, including the times they abused you.

You Will Be Drained and Tapped Out
Narcissists don't like taking the blame for anything. They look for someone else to take the responsibility, and you who have a relationship with one will likely be the one to fill that role. Therefore, to make your relationship work, you will have to come to terms with the fact that you are a scapegoat at every opportunity and probably be demeaned. And if you don't want to take the blame for them, the narcissistic traits will kick in, and they will accuse you of being crazy and inconsiderate. Mostly, all your feelings will be used against you to make you feel bad.

They Will Then Term You a Boring Person
Some narcissists will rather have you keep your job to help keep their lifestyle financed, milking you while you slave for their happiness.
It is a world where time is money and of the essence. Giving time and energy to someone you care about can hold the relationship together. That way, you will have time to fix all the problems that may arise, even if you get blamed.

Remedies to Maintain a Healthy Relationship
You are on the path of managing narcissists. The following tips should be incorporated into your daily dealings with narcissists. With time, narcissists should start getting used to the changes, and possibly, you will notice a difference in them.

"We" Should Be Used as Often as Possible
Whenever possible, try using the word "we," and then strongly emphasize relationships during communications. According to research from Rethinking Narcissism: The Bad—and Surprising Good—About Feeling Special, this simple method works well on narcissists. The study indicates that narcissists were given passages that are filled with words like "our," "we," and "us." When they were done with the course, the narcissists were moved and were willing to help other people in need and became less obsessed with their ideas of being the center of attention.

Reward Good Behavior
Make it a point to observe and compliment the narcissist when you notice they are warm. Give them compliments for their warmth. However, do not praise them for their performance or their achievement. It only makes them want to manipulate and dominate you more.

When you notice they are warm, give them compliments? You can compliment them for being generous, not for their performance or achievement. Be observant and look for moments that the narcissist demonstrates a better behavior and emphasize on it. Pushing a narcissist to the center means highlighting the moments that they show some ability to collaborate, show interest in people, or concern and care for them. Whenever they behave more communal, reward them.

Differentiate Good and Bad Behaviors
When you compliment, does it help? If yes, then you can take it up a notch. It would be best if you tactically contrasted their good behavior with their bad behavior. Determining both actions is more or less like catching, except you recount the past and present the same time. If you do have any of such behavior, note it. It is far more effective when it is contrasted with some recollection of communal behavior.

Let Them Know How You Feel
First and foremost, tell the narcissist how you feel. As you feel unhappy, uneasy, and uncomfortable, use the word "I." For instance, "I am unhappy about your actions." You can use more impactful words like "scared," "afraid," and "sad," but if you are not in a romantic relationship with the narcissist, a less intense language might be better to use. Always go with your gut. The goal here is to describe your experience to narcissists and let them know their behavior that is causing it.

You can let narcissists know how they affect you and how they make you feel. Mention their bad behavior and the likely corrections you want to see.

Understand and Accept Differences
To build a healthy relationship, it is essential that we frankly accept our differences. We need to understand that everyone is unique and different in many ways. If we know that we all perceive the world in different ways, then we might as well have crossed one of the most significant challenges in building relationships.

People often feel better when they think other people understand them and are in tune with their perspective. On the other hand, life would generally be boring and dull if we all think and act the same. Understanding and accepting that we are all wired differently, making us unique, will be a solid foundation for building healthy relationships.

Listen and Pay Attention

Listening while focusing is a skill that improves relationships, perception, and understanding. When you listen and give attention, the other person will feel proud and confident. They will feel supported. They will feel heard. Responsive interactions can promote healthy relationships.

8) Having Children in the Narcissistic Relationship

Knowing what you have learned about narcissism, you might wonder why a narcissist would have a child in the first place. Considering their desire to be taken care of and adored, rather than care for someone and tend to their need, especially a child who needs a great deal of praise and attention.
People have children, whether they are narcissists or not. It doesn't depend on something like that when you and your partner decide to start a family. A narcissist might enjoy having a child or more than one because it creates a close relationship with someone, they will always have power and authority. With the parent-child relationship, the child will always be beneath them because of the nature of their relationship and their difference in age and life experience.
Sadly, and unfortunately, for the narcissist child, they will quickly learn that they exist to please and serve the parent, rather than the parent meeting all of the child's needs first. The narcissist's child serves as a healthy reflection of their accomplishments, achievements, and overall perfection.

Just as narcissistic abuse can occur in a romantic partnership, it can also occur in the parent-child dynamics. A young child with a narcissistic parent will learn that they must act and behave as their parent's reflection, including fitting into behavior and mold of personality dictated by the parent. It can lead to a big deal of anxiety in the child, starting at a very early age. They are persuaded to deny their unique personality to mirror the narcissistic parent who desperately needs them to be.

Failure to comply with the narcissistic parent's wishes, for example, if the child wants to create and set their life goals, the parent will display actions of covert and overt punishment, including avoiding, ignoring, denying, and rejecting the child for a while. The parent will see their child's autonomy as slightly against them as if the child was intentionally betraying them.

A narcissistic parent is hard for a child to understand or trust. They are unpredictable and often confusing, rarely consistent in any direction with their attitudes toward their child or partner. The narcissist is impulsive, surprising, and inconsistent. A child wants stability, trust, and an ability to feel safe as they learn to explore the world.

An inability to understand or make sense of the narcissistic parent's interpersonal "stunts" can lead to the child internalizing feelings of shame, blame, or guilt when they don't live up to the parent's expectations. The child will assume that it is their fault that their parent is unhappy and that they should feel inadequate due to it. A narcissistic parent is entirely oblivious to the harm and damage they are causing their child. The message the child receives is basically, "you are only worthy of love if you comply with my expectations and wishes of you."

Commonly, all of these issues are reflected as the narcissist child grows up and starts attempting to have relationships of their own. In adulthood, they begin to process the trauma of their narcissistic parent caused them as a developing person.

Children of Narcissists as Adults

A distorted child-parent relationship can create many severe emotional and mental issues as you get older and work on having your relationship experiences. Children of narcissists will tend to seek out or gravitate toward challenging or dramatic relationships because it was what was modeled for them as a child. It is what they know love to "look like." Growing up with the belief that you are not nearly excellent or lovable causes only seeking out partnerships that will perpetuate that belief with another partner.

It is relatively common for any child, whether in a narcissistic child-parent relationship or not, to seek out relationships in their adult life that replay what they learned in childhood. Asking for something else feels foreign and strange. Imagine a fish out of the water like a narcissist child receiving unconditional love from a partner, without expecting anything in return. Children of narcissists will seek out romantic partners who are critical or judgmental, emotionally distant or unavailable, or withhold or deny affection and intimacy. Essentially, they will be looking for a partner who feels comfortable and what they know and understand, replaying the dynamics they shared with their narcissistic/codependent parents.

Of course, anyone can heal from such an experience. Sometimes, a child of a narcissist will find that through some therapy and a few healthy partnerships, they can realize, identify, and defy the issues of their childhood experience with their narcissistic parent. Identifying the causes of why you may have problems in your adult relationships often stems from identifying what kind of relationship you had with your early life caregivers.

Often, the child chooses to heal, grow, and move forward from their current relationship. The narcissistic parent will panic and begin to accuse the child of being "brainwashed" or lied to by the therapist/partner/friend/colleague who suggested they help heal their issues. For the parent, this means that they are no longer in control of their child and will have to suffer the consequences of that child's growth and preference to heal the wounds they incurred from the parent-child relationship.

A narcissistic parent might then distance themselves, choosing to reject and deny their child, hoping that their form of punishment will cause their offspring to "see the light" and return to their old dynamic. The parent is very telling in their behavior, as the child can now better see that all their parent wants is to serve their emotional needs and has no feeling for what their child has experienced.

Narcissistic parenting can cause many issues in their child or children, and in adulthood, that child may learn the hard way what they were experiencing with their parent. To break it down further, here is a list of how a narcissistic parent can affect their children:

- The child will feel like they can't be heard or seen.
- They won't have their feelings acknowledged, or their reality validated.
- Rather than being seen as a person, they will be treated as the accessory to the parent.
- They won't be valued for who they are, only for what they can do, especially for the parent.
- The child will develop intense self-doubt, rather than learning to trust themselves and their identity.
- They will learn that how they feel it is less important and how they look is more important.
- They will learn that authenticity is not as good as an image and will learn to be afraid of "being real" with others.
- The child will learn to behave and act secretively as a protection for the family or the parent.
- There will be no healthy encouragement to develop a sense of identity or self.
- They will not feel nurtured and can feel empty of emotions.
- They will learn that it is not right, or dangerous, to trust anyone.
- They will usually feel manipulated or used without understanding the feeling.
- The child will learn to "be there" for the parent, rather than how it should be when the parent is present and available for the child.
- Emotional development is stunted.
- They will feel judgment or criticism instead of unconditional love and acceptance.
- Feelings of not being good enough will develop.
- There will be no role model for creating healthy connections and relationship bonds.
- They will fail to learn healthy boundaries with others.
- They will learn to develop codependency and, therefore, will not learn healthy self-care and self-love.

- They will seek validation from outside of the self instead of learning to validate the self from within.
- They will learn a mixed message of "make me proud" and "don't do anything better than me."
- Will not learn to compliment the self or celebrate the self during essential successes.
- May suffer from depression, addiction, anxiety, or other adulthood issues to cope with childhood trauma.
- Will grow up assuming or believing that they are not lovable or worthy of love because of the parent denying or rejecting them.
- Will grow up with low self-esteem because of the shame in child-parent dynamics.
- They will straddle a life of being someone who self-sabotages, overachieves, or fluctuating back and forth.
- The child will have to learn the hard way how to reparent themselves once they break free from the parent-child dynamics in adulthood.

Being the child of a narcissist is intense, long-lasting, and deeply ingrained into the behaviors, emotions, and even physical qualities and attributes of a person. It can be psychologically and emotionally damaging and can lead to a lifetime of dealing with the programming instilled by the narcissistic parent during their child's formative years.

It can be challenging to tell that someone is a narcissist because of how charming they can be at the moment and how easy it is for them to get slippery as a fish when they are being questioned. They are very cunning, and even some psychologists can miss the red flags when presented with a child's emotional or psychological pain.

Because a narcissist will never claim accountability or responsibility for their actions or behaviors, it then falls upon the child to take the brunt of the blame, guilt, shame, and remorse for anything that goes on. Every situation is different, as every family and individual are different, but the red flags and hallmarks are the same. Assess the above list to see if your child might have some of these symptoms, or if you can identify whether you may have been affected by a narcissistic parent when you were a child.

The opposite of narcissism is empathy. If you are in a situation with a child dealing with a narcissistic parent, then the best way to counter the damaging effects of the narcissist's abuse is to parent with empathy. Offer compassion and support, and help create a secure attachment so that the child in question can experience a healthy love bond that they can carry into their adult life.

It is important to remember that narcissism is a spectrum disorder and takes on varying degrees of severity. Suppose you are a child or co-parenting with a narcissist. In that case, it is essential to understand this disorder so that you can help your whole family in healing, ending patterns and cycles—breaking through to having healthier partnerships and bonds of love for everyone involved.

Whether it is just for the sake of yourself, or perhaps your children as well, depending on the seriousness of the abuse and the effects on your happiness and well-being, letting go and moving on can feel scary. Still, this guide is here to help offer you guidance as you explore and examine your options.

9) Ending A Relationship with A Narcissist

You've accepted you're in a relationship with a narcissist and decided you need to end it. Most relationships with narcissists will have some degree of abuse, however. Emotional abuse will always follow self-centeredness. Whether or not that escalates into the frightening territory or physical abuse varies. How do you end a relationship involving a narcissist? It's a process that can be painful. This guide will help you make that process a little easier and what to expect from the narcissist when they lose you.

What to Do Before Ending the Relationship?

There are certain things you can do beforehand that will better prepare you to make a clean break. These are especially important if you are married or living with your partner, with shared finances. These steps are also crucial if you are being abused and afraid of your partner's reaction to breaking up. Here's what to do:

Cover Your Tracks

Breaking up with a narcissist isn't going to be a smooth process where they respect your decision. They will put up a fight as soon as they find out your plan. Abuse can escalate. As soon as you decide you need to leave, it would be best if you started working towards protecting your privacy. Many abusers monitor their partner's cell phones, emails, and other social media, so they will figure out your plan before you've even really formulated one. Get a second cell phone. Start using another email address to communicate with people about the breakup, especially any lawyers or financial experts. Covering your tracks may seem extreme, but you're dealing with an intense partner. It's okay to be paranoid right now.

Build A Security Net

If you are married or living together, leaving can be incredibly challenging because your partner might have power over your finances and possessions. In abusive relationships, that power will be wielded without mercy. Start building a safety net before your partner gets a chance to take revenge. It includes figuring out a financial plan. Depending on the degree of abuse and situation, this might not be too much of a challenge, but the worst-case scenario would be not controlling any money. If you left, you would be cut off. Talk to friends and family about your situation. Consider a shelter for abuse victims that will give you a place to stay while you figure out further action.

In addition to finances, an abusive narcissist might also have control or access to your documents. Before leaving, you should get copies of your birth certificate, driver's license, passport, any credit cards in your name, health insurance info, etc. If you leave without them, it will probably be tough to get the narcissist to hand them over. Building a safety net is getting your hands on anything and everything you care about, and that's necessary to independence because once you leave, the narcissist will cling to them like a life raft. It's how they keep their power over you.

Gather Emotional Support

Emotional support is just as crucial as getting your finances in order. It's arguably more important because it will keep you focused on reality and your true worth. Without help from trusted friends and family, leaving a narcissist will be extremely difficult. You'll have to fight their manipulation and exploitation alone, and it will be exhausting.

Be cautious about who you share with, however. You don't want to tell someone your plans for breaking up, and then they go and tell your partner.

Sadly, this is not an infrequent occurrence, as narcissists are experts at turning friends against their partners. Not even your family members are automatically immune; there are plenty of stories where an abuse victim's family sides with the abuser. Talk to friends who know what you've been through and who have always been concerned. They will be more than happy that you've seen the light and more than willing to help.

Anticipate Confusing Emotions

While you're developing a plan of escape, you'll feel many emotions, and not all of them will support your desire to leave. Your partner might do something nice for you, and suddenly, you doubt whether things are that bad. That flood of affection triggers pleasant memories, and you wonder if you should give things another shot. It is incredibly tempting if the narcissist isn't abusive, and you're just unhappy.

However, you deserve more than just a "non-abusive" relationship. You deserve true happiness.

When these moments strike, slow down. These conflicting emotions are normal, but they aren't representative of your entire relationship. All of the reasons you had for leaving still stand. Your partner has not suddenly become a different person. When you're preparing to break up with a narcissist, expect these moments of doubt, but accept that's all that they are: moments.

How A Narcissist Reacts to A Breakup?

You've decided it's time to end your relationship. You should know that a narcissist will not respond well. There are particular tactics they'll break out to try and manipulate you into staying. Depending on the person, they might rely on a specific strategy, or use all of them in the hopes something will stick. Here's what to expect:

A Tantrum

Faced with their worst fear, the narcissist will fall apart. They may start crying, throwing things, and just generally losing control. Even if it's subconscious, they're hoping their reaction proves to you how much they need you. They're also hoping to make you feel guilty, so you change your mind. They hope their tantrum translates into, "Look at how much you're hurting me." Please don't fall for it. Keep a cool head, and remove yourself from the situation, especially if you feel unsafe. If the relationship is abusive, it might be best to tell the narcissist you're leaving over the phone, email, or text. It isn't a jerk move if you're doing it to keep yourself safe.

Bargaining

Even people who aren't narcissists will say, "I promise I'll change!" to get their partners to stay. Narcissists, however, are highly unlikely to follow through. "I'll do anything," they say, but really what this means is they will say anything if they think it can manipulate you. If you stick out a relationship with a narcissist after thinking about breaking it off, you may even find they can make some changes. Insults

Like a wounded animal, a narcissist afraid of losing their partner will lash out. They say you're stupid for wanting to break up. In the narcissist's mind, they are perfect, so how could anyone possibly want to leave? They'll break out every degrading thing they ever secretly thought about you, every little thing they know hurts you, and hope that you'll be so broken down, you won't have the strength to leave. "Despite all that's wrong with you, I love you," the narcissist will say, either directly or indirectly, "And no one else ever will." That's a lie, but it's a powerful one. Please don't fall for it.

Closet narcissists might turn their insults towards themselves in the hopes of getting your pity. "I knew it," they'll say, "I'm unlovable." They'll heap on the self-abuse, waiting for you to jump in and comfort them. Ideally, you start telling them all of their great qualities to stem the flow of negativity. You end up convincing yourself why you should stay. It is a trick and doesn't change your original reasons for breaking up.

Threats

Many narcissists rely on threats to get what they want. If they realize you are slipping away, they will do anything to get you to stay. It includes threatening to hurt you directly or indirectly. A direct threat is pretty apparent, but an indirect one would be something like, "You'll regret this because there isn't anybody else like me." They're telling you if you don't stay, you'll end up alone and miserable. While they aren't saying they will cause you bodily or emotional harm, they use fear to manipulate your emotions. The threat of loneliness is scary.

A narcissist may also threaten to hurt themselves. They use your concern for them as a weapon. "If you leave, I'll kill myself," they might say. While this may be a real fear of yours, you cannot stay in a relationship where suicide threats or self-harm are the motivation. It is not your responsibility to treat someone else's mental health.

What If the Narcissist Breaks Up with You?

If the narcissist was the one to end the relationship, there's still a lot of pain involved. They might terminate it suddenly, without much explanation, and vanish from your life. Or, they might lay out all the reasons why they think you aren't good enough and why you never will be. Maybe they cheated and left you for a new partner. Another common tactic is to force you to confront them and break it off. Their heart isn't in the relationship anymore, but they still like the attention and affection they get from you. They'll wonder, either emotionally or sexually. They'll wait for you to notice, so it's up to you to do the emotional labor of ending the relationship. All these scenarios hurt and leave you with a cocktail of emotions - confusion, rejection, grief, and maybe even relief.

The actual reasons for a breakup vary with every relationship, but since the common thread is narcissism, it's most likely because the narcissist wasn't getting the supply they craved. It has nothing to do with you. Narcissists expect way too much and drain the energy from their partners. Even if you feel like you gave them everything, a narcissist will eventually want more. It hurts now, but breaking up, even if it wasn't on your terms, is actually for the best.

10) Divorcing a Narcissist

No divorce in the world is easy; however, divorcing a narcissist can be a terrifying time. You may be worried about the safety and well-being of not only yourself but also your children. If you have decided to divorce your narcissistic spouse, there are some things you need to know. This will lead you to the process of divorce and what you should expect. You will need to find help and create a good defense. We will also know how to deal with a narcissist in court as it is not as cut and dry as other divorce situations.
After realizing that they are married to a narcissist, many people find that the best thing they can do for their overall safety and well-being is to divorce them. It is often the best decision for themselves, as well as their children. Making the decision may be difficult, but it will be better for your children and your children at the end of the day. It takes bravery and knowledge to venture down the road of divorcing a narcissist.
There are a variety of stressors that surround a "normal" divorce. People worry about the financial aspect and the difficulty and pain it causes to everyone involved. Many couples won't ever have to go to court, and they will be able to work it out through mediation and other techniques. When

fighting with a divorce from a narcissist, things are not only more complicated, and you can almost guarantee a judge will end up being involved.

Divorcing a narcissist can become a real mess. People usually work together to stay out of court and find alternatives to the messy process that divorce can entail. When dealing with a narcissist, they will do their best to make things as dirty as possible.

While no one wins in a divorce, the narcissist will strive to feel like they have won. More often than not, when handling divorce, people hope for things to be split down the middle. It includes assets and responsibilities. The narcissist is not going to see it this way at all. They are excellent at playing the victim and will have no intention of meeting you in the middle. They will not take the route of mediation or negotiation.

Their goal will be to be the one seen as being in the right. The truth of a narcissist is anything but truthful.

They will do all means to make themselves look good and sway everyone's opinion, including a judge, to see things from their point of view even if it is tragically skewed.

The narcissist is also a master game player. They have been doing it their whole life, and if you think a courtroom is going to stop this behavior, you are sadly mistaken. They will likely up their game because they are genuinely after a win. They love to hold power, and they do this by keeping other people off-balance. Unfortunately, narcissists tend to be charismatic and charming. It can win favor with a judge or other people involved in your divorce. They will do whatever it takes to wear you down or win the favor of the ones that are making decisions. It makes them dangerous to deal with, especially when kids are involved.

One of the worst things you can do when dealing with a divorce from a narcissist is to throw your hands up in the air and say, "I give up." It is precisely what the narcissist wants. They will ensure this to make it happen. It not only gives them the win but also enables them to feel good about besting you.

They will use this to their advantage with their "friends" and other people to continue making you look bad and making them look like the victim. Stay strong.

You will likely end up in court when divorcing a narcissist as they will refuse to talk reasonable terms.

One of the reasons that the narcissist prefers court is it helps them avoid accountability. When a judge decides, the narcissist is more comfortable as they don't have any responsibility for turning out. Narcissists don't want to be accountable, so the court system can be blamed rather than them whether they win or lose. They also find some illusion of control in putting the decision into the hands of the court.

Planning and Creating of a Secret Account to Fight in Court Against A Narcissist

When dealing with a narcissist, you always want to be proactive. When you are reactive, you are giving them exactly what they want.

There are some things you are certainly going to want to talk with your attorney. You should likely also get a therapist involved. When you have been in a relationship with a narcissist, it takes a psychological toll, so does divorce. The two together can break a person apart, so enlisting a therapist is simply a smart decision. It can help you keep your feelings steady and allow you to be productive while working through this challenging journey.

Talking with a professional can be helpful in many ways. It shows that you are working hard to do your best, and they will be able to give you an unbiased opinion on many things. Remember, you should not be looking for legal advice from your therapist; that is what your lawyer is for. When you are looking for professional support, finding someone specializing in PTSD and narcissistic traits or narcissistic personality disorder will be your best avenue.

Take your time and do your research. Find a lawyer who will handle the extra difficulties that come with dealing with a narcissist. You may have to talk to several attorneys before finding the right one, staying patient, and not being afraid to ask questions. Eventually, you will find the perfect fit to ensure you use the strategies needed to handle a narcissist.

You will also need to take the time to be psychologically prepared. To do this, learn everything you can about narcissism. Learn how to recognize the traits and find the ability to prove that your partner is indeed a narcissist or suffering from a narcissistic personality disorder. You should also seek out a therapist, counselor, or psychologist.

As noted, finding one specializing in narcissistic traits and narcissistic personality disorder will be the most advantageous. If they are also familiar with PTSD, you have found yourself a winner in terms of psychological help. A lot of damage can be done to the partner of a narcissist, and the support of a professional can get you on the right path toward healing and recovering from the abuse you have endured. They can also keep you focused on what is essential.

How a Specialist Divorce Attorney Can Help You
One of the first things you need to do when dealing with a narcissist is to let your attorney know. As stated, narcissists tend to present themselves very well, easily fooling someone who does not know them. They are talented at pulling the wool over the general public's eye.
By letting your lawyer in on who your ex is, you can both be better prepared with how to deal with them.
At least a low rate will show that the narcissist will show their true nature while working through divorce proceedings, but it is just as likely that they will keep their mask in place. When you offer your lawyer the narcissist patterns and how you have dealt with them, it can explain how to deal with him. It leads us to a perfect point when looking for an attorney; it may be best to ask them right upfront if they have ever dealt with a narcissist. If they have not, you should probably keep looking. When you are in such a vulnerable position, making sure the people fighting for you are well-versed in your problems is the best course of action.

Collect Evidence for The Defense in Court
Keeping good records will also work in your favor. From simple conversations that you have with your narcissistic partner to a list of expenditures, all information is useful. When a narcissist starts to play games with the words that were said, you want to prove them wrong. So, being organized and keeping the storyline straight and accurate is a significant bonus to your side of things. This evidence can help show the true nature of your soon to be ex and discredit the ridiculous things that they try and get others to believe.
Maintaining control over your emotions is also going to be a critical element to your success. The narcissist will try to get you angry to act out, which helps give them more power. Do not allow this to happen. Know they are

doing this on purpose to try and gain power and control. Do your best to minimize communication as this will leave less opportunity for you to lose your cool. It would be best if you also kept talking about your spouse to a minimum. It is especially true when it comes to speaking in front of your children or other people that also hang out with your soon to be ex. It may open up a door to the things you are saying, getting back to the narcissist. From there, they will do everything they can to use your words against you. The narcissist will likely try and use their children as pawns. They will try and gain the upper hand in all things through them. It is likely they will even try to turn their children against the other parent. Please do not participate in the same behaviors, and your children will quickly see that you are a trustworthy parent and genuinely care about them. They will also eventually see that the narcissistic parent is merely trying to manipulate them. It can be a difficult situation to face, and you must, above everything else, stay patient and resist the urge to badmouth the narcissist.

No matter how ready you are, there is likely going to be damaged and fallout. It is true of regular divorces, so it is even more real when dealing with a narcissist divorce.

You will be facing high levels of stress, and it will be a test of your endurance. When children are added to this mix, it only makes it more challenging. Know that it is not impossible; you need to be prepared. Take the time to prepare truly. Take notes of what has transpired throughout your relationship and be prepared to talk about all of the horrible things that have occurred. Note the help of your friends and family so that you have the emotional support that you need.

11) Do Not Change Your Mind and Remember your Motivation

We're covering a lot of information that you need to know when divorcing a narcissist specifically. Still, at this halfway point of the process, there is one thing you need to remember and remind yourself of - never change your mind.

Your ex is very likely to throw everything at you during the divorce proceedings, and at the point when you inform them of what you want, you must hold firm. As you move through the process, there is likely to be a nagging doubt enters your mind at some stage. Please do not listen to it

If you change your mind and call off the divorce at this point, your partner is going to make your life a literal living hell. They will not take anything you say seriously at that point, if they ever did before, they will never let you forget the perceived injustice that you attempted to impart on them. There is very unlikely to be any joyful times from that point onwards.

Remember Your Primary Motivation

Remember the reason you wanted the divorce in the first place. What was it that triggered you and made you make that decision? What was the lightbulb moment?

Remember it, pull it to the front of your mind, and commit it to your memory. Note it down and read it regularly if you need to, but this is something you must remember at all times. Your primary motivation for leaving is the point that tipped you over the edge and made you suddenly realize that you deserve better. That is a joyous moment for you, something which urged you to act and leave a situation that caused you nothing but pain and confusion, even if you didn't realize it wasn't your fault at the time. When things get tough when your partner starts to throw everything, including the kitchen sink, your way, when they try and convince everyone that you're lying and they're perfect, visualize that moment you decided that you wanted a divorce. Remember how it felt when you suddenly realized that you don't have to deal with this anymore.

It is useful for you to meditate and try and pull the exact moment to their minds. A visualization is a potent tool, and it can help you remember the reasons you made your decision. That reason hasn't changed and hasn't gone away; it's buried underneath a lot of confusion and pain, the typical situation that occurs in the middle of a divorce. The only difference with a divorce from a narcissistic that you're likely to feel even more confused because the gaslighting doesn't end.

Turning on The Charm

There are two main ways a narcissist will deal with the divorce, so let's look at those in turn.

Firstly, they might turn on the charm. If they don't do this thoroughly, they will use this tactic periodically throughout the divorce process. It is designed to make you remember the good times and therefore think twice about continuing with the divorce.

They will suddenly go back to the person they were when you first met when everything was beautiful, and you felt like you had met the most fantastic person in the world. Remember, they are not that person; in reality, they are acting, and everything they are showing you is nothing but an act. It is a form of emotional abuse because the sole aim is to make you fall in love repeatedly and not want to end the connection you have. The problem is, once they see that you've chosen to stay in the relationship and not go through with the divorce, they're going to go back to the way they were before, if not worse. Probably worse.

Abuse Coming Your Way

The other possibility is that a constant stream of abuse is going to come your way instead. It could work with the charm, but at some point, the abuse will give way, and you'll be subjected to constant lies, passive-aggressive behavior, insults, and making you look like the bad guy.

In some ways, while the abuse is terrible and upsetting, it's less likely to make you want to go back to your partner! It could be too damaging your self-esteem and make you think about things that happened in the past. The gaslighting which narcissists are known for could also cause us to believe that certain events were your fault when they most certainly were not.

It's vital that you're prepared for both sides of the coin, but also that you remember your reason for wanting a divorce in the first place, and keep that in your mind when you might start to waver and wonder whether this entire process is what you want.

If you hadn't wanted it ultimately, you wouldn't have made the decision. Any thoughts on changing your mind are firmly down to how your ex manages the situation themselves and their behavior towards you. Take them out of the equation from this point onwards and focus entirely on yourself instead. That is the best way to deal with it all.

However, you should recognize that having second thoughts during any divorce is normal, but it doesn't mean you should change your mind. You shared feelings at some stage, and you were in love enough to marry them in the first place. Of course, it's going to be hard, and you're going to wonder whether you're doing the right thing, but when it comes to getting away from a narcissistic relationship, you're always doing the right thing.

12) Division of Finance

Determining how to divide your finance or assets in a divorce requires the same type of analysis as deciding whether you or your spouse will need spousal support after the divorce. The first thing you need to do is get the facts. That means you need to figure out what you have, what you owe, and what you need. Only then can you divide what you've got in a way that makes sense.

It is similar to doing a budget, only instead of listing your income and expenses, you are listing your assets and your debts. It would be best if you listed things as completely as possible in a way that makes sense to you so that you can clearly and easily see what you and your spouse have to divide. Writing a list of your assets and liabilities is fine—if you know what you have. What if you don't know what your assets or your debts are? What if you've never been good with numbers, so you just let your spouse deal with all of the money issues during your marriage? What if your spouse was the controlling sort and never let you see any of your financial information?

Worse yet, what if your spouse always hid that type of information from you? It's simple—you have to figure it out!

Finding and compiling financial information may be tedious, but it's not brain surgery. If you are the same with most people, you have access to all the information you need—you have to look at it. Open your mail, go to your bank, dig out copies of your tax returns, and talk to your financial advisor. Ask your employee benefits department for copies of your retirement account information. Find your recent credit card statements. If you can't find any statements, see if you can get them online, or call the credit card companies and get copies of the statements sent to you (preferably at an address other than your home in case your spouse intercepts your mail). Call the credit bureaus or go online and get a copy of your credit report. Do whatever you can to get the information you need—including asking your spouse for it! Believe it or not, sometimes it is that simple. Sometimes it's not, but it never hurts to try.

Finding Hidden Assets

Like most people, gathering financial information is a pretty dull, but relatively simple task. You all need to open the file cabinet, sort through mountains of paperwork, and figure out what you need. However, if your narcissist spouse has been purposely hiding money or other assets from you, you can search the entire house and still not find the papers you need to tell you what you have. If you find that's true for you, you will have to do a lot more than look through your bank statements to get a fair shake in your divorce.

Before you automatically assume that your narcissist spouse is hiding money from you, you need to determine whether that assumption is based in reality or is just a part of typical divorce paranoia. To do that, ask yourself a few questions. Have you been actively involved in your finances during your marriage? Do you have a general awareness of the value of the things you own and what you owe? Is your narcissist spouse an employee who gets a paycheck every week? Did you and your spouse file a joint income tax return every year while you were married? Do you have access to all of your financial information?

If yes, chances are, no matter how paranoid you might feel, your narcissist spouse is probably not hiding money from you. That's not to say that your spouse couldn't have stashed away a little nest egg somewhere. However, if you've paid attention to money during your marriage and know how much comes in and goes out every month, there is probably not too much your spouse could have hidden from you. If you've been financially clueless throughout your marriage, if your narcissist spouse is self-employed or works for cash; or, if your spouse has never shared any financial information with you, you might have a problem.

Suppose you reasonably suspect that your spouse is hiding money from you. In that case, the first thing you need to do is gather as much information about your finances—and your spouse's finances—as you possibly can, given the situation you are working with. Do everything you would do even if your spouse weren't hiding information—open your mail, go through your file cabinets, find your tax returns, and dig out the buried documents in the back of your closet. Even if your spouse has been purposely trying to hide information, you will still be amazed at what you can find if you look.

If you need to hire an attorney, an accountant, or a private investigator to help you, do it. Just understand that the more information you can put together yourself, the better off you're going to be, and the less money you will have to spend. You're also probably in a much better position to find information than your attorney, as you're the one who gets your family's mail, voice mail, and email.

No matter how much you dig to find your financial information and figure out where your money is, there are two circumstances in which your spouse can effectively hide money from you with relative ease and probably without getting caught. If your husband owns a business, there are a hundred ways to make sure the business doesn't show a profit or appears to suddenly be losing money while he or she is going through a divorce. Unless you are willing to hire a forensic accountant and spend tens of thousands of dollars on business valuations and business analysis, you will never be able to find everything your spouse has hidden.

What To Do After You Know What You Have?

The most productive way to divide up your assets is to use your head, not your heart. Use common sense. Take your list of assets and liabilities, and ask yourself, "What do I want? What do I need? What does my spouse want? What is fair?" Most people will claim they don't care what their spouses want and prefer that their spouses don't get whatever they want anyway. However, if that's the approach you take to dividing your property, you will be fighting over nonsense for a very long time. Divorce is emotional enough. Fighting over the silverware helps no one. Try to be objective and fair, and be realistic. If you can barely afford your house payments on what you and your spouse make together, what makes you think you will be able to make those payments on your salary alone? Yes, you may love the house, and yes, you may want to keep it. But you can't afford it. So, sell it, divide the proceeds, and be done with it.

When it comes to dividing your debt, the same principles apply. The more you can keep your emotions out of your decisions, the better off you will be. Because joint debt will follow both of you, it makes sense to get rid of as much of your combined debt as you can. It also makes sense to divide as much of your other debts as possible based upon whose name those debts are in. If all the debts are in your name, that's not going to work. However, if your credit card bills and your spouse's credit card bills are about the same, it makes sense for you to keep the bills in your name and for your spouse to keep the bills in his or her name. Doing that is just easier. It's also more comfortable, and makes more sense, for the spouse who keeps a piece of property to keep whatever debt is associated with that piece of property. If you own the car, you should also keep the car loan. If you can't afford the loan, then either your spouse should take the car, or you should sell it, pay off the debt, and buy a car that you can afford.

Dividing your assets and liabilities is difficult, not just because you're dealing with money, but because you're dealing with your emotions about money and your feelings about your marriage, divorce, and soon-to-be-ex. The more you can divide your feelings from what you're doing and approach your property division as you would approach a business deal—rather than treating it as just another fight with your spouse—the better off you will be. Follow your head, take control of your heart, and you will be in the best position to negotiate a deal that you can live with in the future. Just remember— in the end, it is only money.

13) Dealing with Co-Parenting with a Narcissist

What if you end a relationship with a narcissist, but have children together? It complicates the situation, but it isn't hopeless. Your child can still grow up healthy and happy; you will have to be the responsible, consistent figure in their lives

You know what it's like to be a narcissist's partner, but what about a child? It's essential to understand what your kid is going through if their other parent - your ex - is a narcissist. Depending on how long you were with your ex with a child or children in the mix, you've probably noticed the unhealthy aspects of their parenting style.

Like their partner, a narcissist won't pay attention to what their child needs or wants. The narcissist's needs always take priority, so the child learns from a young age that what they want doesn't matter. They are never nurtured and taught to feel safe. They feel small and insignificant. Your children may not even know how to express what they want and need because that type of thinking has never been encouraged. Their sense of self can be very stunted. To counter this messaging, encourage your child to pursue their dreams. Ask them questions about how they feel and what they think about things, whether it's movies, friendships, or your ex's separation. If your kid expresses a lot of insecurity and self-doubt, gently guide them to feel like they have support and freedom. This guidance can be applied to finding a hobby or having conversations about their feelings about their lives.

Narcissists frequently put very high expectations on their kids. They believe their kids reflect on them, so they push them to succeed. The child won't feel loved unless they're doing something well, looking a certain way, or thinking certain things. The narcissist might be very critical, judgmental, and withholding when their kid inevitably "fails." The child will feel like nothing they do is ever good enough. It's widespread for these kids to have low self-esteem and very poor self-worth because they believe love is conditional. Pushing back against the belief that love is conditional is arguably the most important thing you can do as a parent. Parents should always be the people a child can rely on for love, no matter what. If your ex isn't capable of being that, it's more important that you take on that role wholeheartedly. Always celebrate your child, mostly when they "fail" or don't meet your ex-set expectations. Let them know your love isn't dependent on their successes; you love them because of who they are, not what they do. You can still encourage them to improve and set goals, but never attach your attention and affection to an outcome. Be sure to tell them you love them no matter what, too. Words are powerful.

When you get upset, don't lose control around your kid. That includes any strong emotions, like grief or anger. However, it would be great to inspire your kid to express those emotions when they need to. Be a shoulder to cry on and a safe place. When they get angry, help them figure out healthy ways of expression instead of punishing them. They'll see that you are emotionally stable and nurturing, even when their other parent can't be.

If your narcissist ex wants to be involved in your children's lives, there are certain things you can do to make the process easier and safer.

Set Communication Boundaries

As a co-parent, you will need to talk to your ex. However, you can decide when you speak and about what. Your ex will always try to push the boundaries and use any opportunity to get under your skin. They may even try to get you so angry that you lose control, which gives them leverage over you. Avoid talking on the phone or in-person if your ex likes to go on rants, emotionally abuse you, or try to get you worked up. Stick to emails, which give you more control over what you say, and it keeps everything in writing. It's impossible to control what your ex says when your kid is with them. However, when the kid is with you, you can set more boundaries. Expect your ex to want to talk to the kid a lot. Set a schedule and stick to it. For example, no phone call on school nights after 8 pm, and only after homework. Your ex will probably try to break these rules, so stand your ground. If you believe your ex uses phone calls to emotionally abuse your child or disregard any other agreements made in court, consider recording them. In many places, you must tell your ex their call is being recorded. Talk to a lawyer before moving forward.

If things are too complicated and challenging, get a parent coordinator. Judges appoint these people, and they act as a mediator between you and your ex, so you don't need to talk to them unless necessary. The parent coordinator handles scheduling visits and any other communication.

Protect Your Child

If your co-parent has custody or visitation rights, it's hard to control what your ex says. Never used your child as a messenger pigeon. Please don't ask them to communicate with your ex on your behalf or ask them to spy. It puts the kid in a very awkward and possibly scary situation. You can find out how they're being treated and what they're doing just by having regular conversations. If you're concerned by something they say, ask them a question like, "How does that make you feel?" There are certain things your child might not want to talk about with you, so getting your kid to counseling is an excellent idea.

Be especially aware of how your child's milestones might affect your ex. As healthy kids get older, they will become more independent. Narcissists typically resist this aspect of child-rearing because they want to keep control. You will feel many emotions, especially negative ones, during a co-parenting scenario with a narcissist. But don't use your child as a sounding board for your frustrations with your ex. It not only makes the kid feel like they need to comfort you and manage your feelings; it makes them think torn about their love for their other parent. They might instinctively resist your criticisms, jump to your ex's defense, or become angry and even scared of their other parent. It puts them in your ex's crosshairs while also making mad at you for turning their child against them. The already-fragile co-parenting situation becomes even more volatile and stressful for your child.

The Most Written Detail, the Best

Co-parenting with a narcissist is complicated, and every situation is a little different. The best-fitting you can do is to keep detailed records. Right at the beginning, when you start seeing a family law attorney, tell them what's going on with your ex. Tell them they are a narcissist and are "high-conflict," a legal term for these custody scenarios. In your custody agreement, write down every detail, like who pays for what, the days and times they have visitation, holiday visitations, and more.

Having detailed records is also essential as life continues because your ex is unlikely to follow the rules peacefully. They will try to push back, and having forms of their lousy behavior protects you and your children. If they cancel or try to move around visitation, write it down. If they refuse to pay for something or are late with the money, write it down. Using phone calls to manipulate your kid? Tell them that you would record the call. Any communication between you two should be saved, if possible. This evidence lets you hold them accountable.

Take Care of Yourself

Self-care is not selfish. As a parent, this has never been truer. If you let yourself get drained, worn down, and depleted, you'll have nothing to offer your kid. You'll have less patience, less stability, and more irritability. Your kid won't come to you because they'll see how exhausted you are, and they won't want to burden you. Not only will you not have the physical or emotional energy to care for them, but you're modeling unhealthy habits they will imitate. They won't know how to take care of themselves and like you, and they'll burn out. For both your sake and the sake of your kids, practice good self-care.

Find a Community

Your child may fundamentally lack a second parent, but that doesn't mean you're in this alone. Don't burden yourself by believing you are your kid's only adult role model. Find a community that supports both you and your child and rich with healthy, loving people who can encourage your child's emotional growth. A society can also help you by giving your friends vent to, happy to babysit, and more. People need community, especially when life gets rough.

Don't Let Your Ex Manipulate You

One of the best things you can do is not let your ex infect you with toxic thoughts and beliefs to be a good parent. As you know, they will use your child as a weapon. Expect to hear things like, "How could you do this to our family?" They will try to make you guilty for leaving and say that the separation is bad for your children. When they see you aren't budging, they'll move on to the custody agreement, and say, "That's bad, too." Please don't believe it. They will be just as critical and selfish in their relationship with their child as they were with you, so leaving and sticking to a particular arrangement is the only healthy thing.

Your ex probably won't stay quiet about their frustrations and trash you on social media and anyone who will listen. Having people, even friends, believe you are a terrible parent can be challenging. Keep a standing firm, and remember that this is what's best for your child. The people who know you will be supportive.

14) How to Protect Your Children From A Violent Narcissistic Father

After you have divorced a narcissist, you are still going to be facing many challenges. When children are involved, those challenges become even more difficult. Your children will need help learning how to cope with divorce and dealing with the damage their narcissistic parent has caused. Things with a narcissist are never easy, and they have a detrimental impact on your children. Learning different strategies to heal and cope will be necessary to ensure they lead healthy and fulfilling lives.

There is a lot of legal advice given to parents who have gone through a divorce and have children involved; unfortunately, this advice is not going to work or apply to those who divorced a narcissist. Trying to co-parent with a narcissist is almost impossible. You will, more often than not, be working on reducing conflict. At this point, you realize that narcissists love drama and will do anything they can to provoke you and even your children to keep playing their games of control and manipulation.

To protect your children from their narcissist father, what you need to do is refuse to engage with them, especially when their behavior is inappropriate.

The narcissist will try for all attention, and whether it is negative or positive, it does not matter. So, shutting down the opportunity by disengaging will work well in favor of both you and your children.

Disengaging with a narcissist can be a scary thing. In theory, it should be easy, but as you well know, there is nothing easy when you have a narcissist to deal with. When they realize what you are doing, it could escalate. They may become volatile. The best thing you can do is stand your ground. Eventually, the narcissist will realize that they cannot provoke you into a battle, and they will move on to another target. You must be patient and strong through the process.

When you try to disengage and keep the peace between you and the narcissistic father, you need to remember that conversations with them need to be minimal. You will need to talk to them about matters concerning the kids, but that does not mean you need to talk about anything else.

You may think that keeping them away from their father is the best course of action, but realistically kids need both parents. Your children love both of you even if one doesn't give it back to them in healthy ways. They need to see their father and make decisions regarding them for themselves. If you restrain, you will likely do more harm than good. You may even end up with children that resent you because they can't understand why you would put a stop to their relationship with their father. You must sit back and allow them to figure out their narcissistic father on their own.

The emotions they will go through while dealing with their narcissistic father will be like riding a roller coaster. So, the more structure they have with you, the better off they will be. You can provide them with a sense of safety and balance, which they will need to continue to lead healthy lives.

You also want to be careful about how you handle your children, and you should do your best not to feel sorry for them. Sure, growing up with a narcissistic father is not going to be an easy thing, but there are worse situations in which they could find themselves. When we pity our children, it helps enable them to take on a victim complex, and this can be detrimental to them as they grow. When you have the mentality that you are a victim, it tends to stop you in your tracks, making moving past the problem insanely tricky. Additionally, they are more apt to end up in toxic relationships rather than searching for healthy ones.

Your narcissistic ex will likely become emotionally intense from time to time. They will try and goad you into getting on this ride with them, but you must refrain and consider the impact all of this has on their children. Instead of playing the narcissist's game, you need to stay calm, non-emotional, and pleasant. It will be a challenging thing to do, but you have to do your best. Practicing things like mindfulness, deep breathing, and meditation can help you find balance and calmness more easily.

Making sure your children can traverse this tumultuous past, you are going to have to let go a little bit. It means you should limit the amount of texting and contact you have with your kids while they are with their other parent, and your ex should do the same when they are with you. If there is an emergency, you should feel free to reach out, but other than that; you should both allow uninterrupted time with the children.

If your children are contacting you about every little thing that your ex is doing, it will cause you a lot of stress and make the situation even more difficult.

When you allow your children to assert themselves to their narcissistic father, it helps them to cope with the situation and learn how to deal with difficult people throughout their entire lives.

You will be benefiting your kids in a significant way if you teach them about emotional intelligence. Additionally, it would be best if you practiced what you preach to help them understand and learn it even more. When you can give them examples of some prosperous single-family households, they can understand how the situation they are currently in should be. Helping your kids understand how to regulate their emotions and cope with the difficult things in life early is a good thing.

When you're talking to your children, you need to keep it age-appropriate. Still, straightforward communication is the best way to talk to kids, especially if their other parent is a narcissist as their emotional intelligence will be extremely low.

When dealing with a narcissistic, you need to remember that they will never nurture your children's uniqueness and independence. They will likely be unable to focus and see your children as individuals they have needs and feelings. Instead, they look at their children as an extension of themselves. The narcissist will probably feel as if emotional growth from the child is selfish, and they will respond with a variety of destructive behaviors. Unfortunately, your children will likely try and find approval from their narcissistic father by meeting the narcissist sets' unrealistic requirements. Whether you feel your children are ahead of the game in terms of maturity or not, you need to be careful that you are not criticizing their other parent while they are around. Psychologically understanding a narcissist is extremely difficult, and regardless of your child's maturity level, you should not put that on them. It complicates things even more so than they already are. What you know to be true of the narcissist in your life may be completely different from society's views. Additionally, your children likely see them in a very different light than you do, so keeping your feelings to yourself will ensure that they do not sustain harm from your side of the fence.

When you are parenting children, who have a narcissist in their lives, you need to be very careful. As you likely remember, your ex was probably prone to angry outbursts that can lead to emotional devastation. Your children don't need these angry outbursts from each side, so staying in control of your anger and what you say when you feel less than stellar is extremely important in showing them they have a reliable, safe place to express themselves with you.

Active listing and then reflective communication can also help your children feel validated and understood. Their struggle and pain are genuine, and showing them that you can see it will help them cope with it. Please do your best to tune into their hearts by looking them in the eyes when you are speaking and simply being near them when you know they are feeling down. In time, your children will likely realize that their narcissistic father looks at them as if they are an object, not a human being. It is heartbreaking and devastating. More than likely, you have experienced this moment with your narcissistic acts, as well. It would be best if you understood how difficult this is to accept. You will not be able to treat this pain away from your children, but you can provide them with the comfort and support they need to grieve and work their way through it. Don't be afraid to grieve with them. You have all suffered from a loss and need to work together to move on.

They need a place and a parent to provide them with warmth, love, stability, strength, flexibility, and solace. All of the narcissist's tactics like gaslighting, emotional abuse, and invalidation used to be focused on you, and unfortunately, once you divorce the narcissist, they will start to focus these things on your children. Remembering the time and what it was like when you went through these negative experiences will help you relate and care for your children as they go through it.

Another way to help ensure that your children grow into well-rounded individuals is to learn how to love.

The narcissistic father will show them that they have to perform in a certain way or earn love, which is precisely the opposite pattern of thinking that you want them to have. Through your actions, you can show them how to care about people by being compassionate and kind rather than selfish and shortsighted. You can never count on the narcissistic parent to lead by example, which means you must always keep it at the forefront of your mind so that you do.

Watch for signs of abuse. Physical, mental, and emotional abuse are entirely unacceptable, and if you notice any of them occurring, you need to take immediate action. Unfortunately, emotional and mental abuse are common occurrences when dealing with a narcissist. Finding a way to protect your children from this can be not easy, especially if there are custody arrangements already in place. If your children are emotionally, physically, or mentally abused, you should reach out to your attorney and talk about what options are available to you.

Keep in mind that if you have to take your narcissistic ex back to court, it will likely be extremely challenging. They will use all of the same tactics that they used before to try and get you back into their web of chaos.

Stay calm and continue pushing forward with the intent of providing your children with the safety they deserve.

15) The Psychological Consequences After A Toxic Relationship

Unbelief, discomfort, anger, grudge are the classic expressions after abandonment from a narcissist. Many women stay with the hope of a comeback of their ex, denying the end of the relationship, "he loves me, it's not possible that is over, he will come to me again, it's just a period, he didn't leave me for real, he just wants to punish me for something, he will come back, and we will be happy."

Many naïve girls, hoping that the relationship could continue, try to get in touch with the narcissist in social networks or make him jealous hanging out around his place, going there with a friend, and pretending to be lovers. To the eyes of a narcissist, you will appear more stupid and childish.

Many women suffer for five or six months, destroyed from the toxic relationship sharply ended. Suppose the narcissist shows up again (which systematically does) while the women are still in this state of suffering for the loss. She will likely fall again under the perverted narcissist's manipulation. By still nourishing hopes to repair the relationship and still

being in love with the man who made her suffer, she will harm herself for real this time. A narcissist's enjoyment in these returns is remarkable.
He mistreated and abandoned the victim without reason, and she's still there desiring him. This situation is a substantial narcissistic refueling.
After the umpteenth abandonment, the victim will feel angry and thirsty for revenge.
But meanwhile, our narcissist already unleashed his "flying monkeys" to vilify the victim's reputation. The term "flying monkeys" is indicated the people who help the narcissist in his defamation campaigns.
The victim not getting revenge or finding comfort and support in other people will move from rage to desperation. In the most severe forms, the vilified and abandoned person will develop depression and a sense of emptiness.

Being Able To Accept
Accepting that a relationship is over or the beloved person was perverted will allow you to overcome the period of discomfort and face new relationships with better awareness. It's a conscious decision. It's useless to dream that things will change, staying still, and passive in front of life's challenges. Knowing how to accept is necessary to have a capacity for self-determination.
The Buddha taught us that everything is impermanent, so it's pointless to get attached to "things," mostly if they result from our thoughts. Don't stay anchored to suffered injustices and natural feelings of revenge; move the mental focus on the future. Our mind will be a prisoner of such harmful thoughts by fixing negative elements, taking us in a descendant spiral of hate and anguish.
An aware capacity of acceptance will give you the strength to start over.

Starting Over
The first thing is to learn your mistakes and transform them into lessons. After being betrayed, cheated, and manipulated, it's not that easy to get out of abandonment. You will be afraid and defensive, but know that not everyone is perverted or egoist, empathic, and altruist.
If you need to let off steam, do it with your close friends and never on a first date with a new person.

Avoid generalizing, starting to believe that men are "all the same"; generalizations indicate a cognitive disorder.

Obviously, before going out with a new person, take the necessary time to metabolize the ex-traumatic story completely. Don't let yourself be caught from the rush, in the hope to compensate the pain with a new love story. You never choose the right thing in a hurry.

If you need to hang out with people, group meetings will be the best thing. Also, committing at work will create benefits, moving the focus from past pain to future commitments.

After periods of defeats and sufferings, many women end with the past "cut" their hair as a renovation sign. It is the moment to find again the motivation to live fully and return to social life. This opening period will give you the chance of new meetings, even if your goal is to socialize, returning to a normal lifestyle.

Mistrust And Expiration

After a traumatic sentimental experience, many people, either male or females, mature a hyper distrust towards the opposite sex. It is a typical defensive attitude that has to take you to prudence and not to psychotic forms, generically mistrusting everyone.

Not so young women feel pressed to choose quick and fair. Such a necessity is harmful and will bring intense disappointments. To have extreme needs, like finding the love of life within two years, will make you fall again in some chronic liar or serial seducer's arms. Even if you are lucky finding ordinary people, having an excessive expectation (marriage, children, happiness, financial security) on the person you are dating, you won't stand a natural consumption of the relationship. Birth, consumption, and end of a relationship is the natural and standard loop in most sentimental experiences. Finding the right person is possible, but you can't organize it, deciding status and time to fall in love and get married. The meeting between two people is a magic that happens in unlikely places and moments when the rational choice leaves the place to an open meeting and without social masks. To unmask to the other doesn't mean to be gullible and be tricked by a fake and manipulative person (narcissist), but being yourself to get in the intimacy of souls (essence). Intimacies like these are rare, but they happen at least a couple of times in life. For the less fortunate, remember that a healthy relationship is also fulfilling and full of love.

Remember that a relationship must be nourished daily with attention, acts, and presence to be long-lasting. The mutual esteem and consideration are the concrete of a relational construction.

The Way Of Happiness

Focus on what you want. Instead of following necessities induced by society or being conditioned by parents, focus on what you want. Few have clear ideas on what they want, and to know it imagines to be at your funeral. Imagine it with all the details, who is there, married, children, and how many, what you left. This image of the scene of your funeral will make you aware of what is essential for you. Maybe you want a large family or having done important things, having a love of your friends and relatives, having been a good husband, becoming an engineer, etc.

Many people are horrified by the scene they imagined, finding themselves in front of a funeral with four people, without a girlfriend or wife crying for his passing. If you don't like the scene, you still have time to change it. Either the setting is positive or negative will indicate what you want, or you will be more aware. Once you are aware of what you want to achieve in life, focus on such goals. Critical goals are long-term, so to realize them, divide them into small steps. Without losing sight of the plan, start to work and act on the first step. Don't make you distract from the past, sufferings, or overthinking about time wasted; focus on the present or future.

Don't let yourself be discouraged from difficulties or defeats; they are part of your life and are necessary to make yourself more substantial and more aware in the future.

Behave ethically and be an example of who is close to you, especially your children. A person responsible for his behavior will create harmony around him. Always maintain promises; if you don't feel like doing something or commit in relationships or projects, say it frankly. No one is forced to do what he doesn't want or doesn't feel like to do. Many people say yes to everything and everyone, without maintaining the commitment. These disturbed people spoil relationships and harmony in their range of motion. Please don't do like them; it's your right to say no, but you have to be responsible once you commit. Responsibility is necessary to acquire real happiness in life. Some people believe they are clever, tricking, or not making their commitments. These people consider being "smart." Such behaviors will bring them misfortune.

The responsible person is the only one that can be free; freedom without responsibility doesn't exist.

16)   Lasting Effects

What happens after you're able to leave the relationship, either willingly or unwillingly?

No matter what happens in the end, it's likely you still won't have closure or satisfaction that it's over. You'll realize that even though you've ended the worst part of the journey, you're about to embark on the second-worst: the road to recovery and finding yourself again.

This guide is about what happens after the relationship ends, and what you might have to deal with psychologically and emotionally. After all, if someone has been beaten either mentally or physically, there must always be a recovery period.

It's easier with physical scars because almost everything will heal with time, and it's plain to see if you're healthy or not. You may have a scar or several, but they fade over time, and you can even forget that you were injured. However, with emotional and mental wounds, it's much more difficult. If you don't actively address them, they won't heal on their own. Instead, they'll grow and fester inside the longer you wait, and they'll manifest in ways that you won't understand. Time does not heal these wounds, and however much you want to move on and tuck those memories away immediately, you can't, for your good.

You opened your heart and trusted someone, and all they did was take advantage and stomp on it. You might not have realized it, but it fundamentally changed how you view the world and its people. There can be ripple effects that you probably don't realize until years after.

You might believe that the world isn't out to get you, that people are generally good-hearted, that you can control your own life, and that you are generally a good person of value and worth knowing.

An abusive relationship can shatter all of these inherent beliefs because your abusive relationship has proven them false. If you don't believe that if you behave and treat others well, you will reap the benefits of those inherent assumptions, then what motivation do you have to do anything? How can you control your fate and happiness? Can you at all?

If you do everything right with the best of intentions only to be held hostage by an abusive partner, life truly seems pointless. You can see how this would be a difficult mindset to rebuild from.

So, what happens after the relationship ends?

After effect #1: You will likely be suspicious and distrusting of any member of the gender of your abuser. You might even cultivate bitterness and hatred towards them, even if you are a member. You aren't sure that you can trust anyone, and you won't open yourself up to anyone. You also distrust your assessment skills because of your past abusive relationship. You may have an overall discomfort with new people and especially with those that show romantic interest in you.

Aftereffect #2: You may have flashbacks, in the sense that you will suddenly be taken to a prior traumatic event from your abusive partner. It will feel like it just happened and will be fresh and new in your memory. You will almost be able to taste and smell it. Your anxiety and alertness will be correspondingly high. You may have specific triggers that bring flashbacks on, or it might be a general sense of anxiety that occasionally flares up into something more. These are traumatic memories.

After effect #3: Like flashback triggers, you might have negative reactions to common, everyday things you can't explain. The reason is these everyday things, occurrences, events, and locations remind you of your abuser, and when you think of your abuser, you immediately go into a dark, hurt place. Everything comes pouring back to you in a second, and you feel like you're still with your abuser.

After effect #4: You may obsess and fixate over the relationship. Not over your partner, but over what you did and how, and when things unraveled. You constantly find instances in which to blame yourself and then dissect what you could have done better. No one says that you need to forgive and forget immediately, but obsessing is the inability to let go and move on – to release yourself from the mental burden of thinking about the abuse.

After effect #5: Some people may feel compelled to grab their newfound free will and essentially lose control. They feel that they've been under someone's thumb for so long, and been told what to do, that they want to experience the exact opposite. They can become unstable, compulsive, impulsive, and spontaneous to the point of danger. It seems like a way of taking back their power and free will, but unfortunately, it can be self-damaging. It also doesn't address the underlying feelings of resentment and hurt.

After effect #6: You may be in a state of constant anxiety or sensitivity. The smallest thing can rile you up and alarm you, and cause you to panic. It's because the smallest things recently caused outbursts from your abusive partner, so you're accustomed to never feeling like you can be safe and let your guard down. Therefore, you don't. You're in constant fight, and this is both mentally and physically exhausting. You're also extremely irritable and prone to emotional outbursts as a result of being on edge.

After effect #7: Very frequently, you will experience signs of posttraumatic stress disorder (PTSD), and the more specific posttraumatic relationship disorder (PTRD).

Let's dive into After Effects #7 with more detail because it is a serious condition that, just like abuse, people don't want to believe, it happens to them. But it does and can, so awareness and education are extremely important.

Posttraumatic Stress Disorder

Better known as PTSD – what does it mean, though? Usually, you'll only hear this term to soldiers that return from war because of the horrors they have seen.

PTSD can broadly apply to anyone that has experienced traumatic events. PTSD generally causes people to relive the event mentally, with memories surfacing unpredictably and crippling fear and anxiety. People with PTSD show "hyperarousal" and are suspicious of anything that is not immediately within their control. Being constantly on guard for the upcoming attack is exhausting.

Technically, the type of PTSD that would apply to abuse victims is called complex post-traumatic stress disorder. It pertains to a wider type of trauma and stress, over a longer period, like an abusive relationship.

A new category of PTSD has also risen to prominence, and it is called posttraumatic relationship syndrome (PTRS). It directly addresses the consequences of someone that has been subjected to domestic or emotional abuse.

How do you deal and heal, even if you have PTRS?

The first step is undoubtedly making sure that you are 100% clear of the situation and safe from any future recurrences. It often means removing yourself physically and cutting off all contact. The main thrust here is to feel safe and let your guard down slightly, and realize that you aren't subject to imminent attack anymore. When you feel safe, you also find stability. It's impossible to be stable if your world can be flipped in a split second.

For many, getting back into our daily routines and reconnecting with friends and family is a large part of feeling safe. What's more, feeling a sense of normalcy is also important, like you didn't get granted parole from your prison. You want to set up new routines and be able to set aside old ones that were dictated by your abuser. That's the first place where you can also exercise your power and free will.

Second, it's undoubted that you must begin to process the trauma you went through and what happened. Don't feel a need to rush to this stage, as some people can take years to do this, and others can take weeks. Some people might be able to do this with their friends, and others might need professional help for years, depending on what happened.

It's important to start thinking about the fact that you were sucked into someone else's reality, and that everything you believed was not true. It was an elaborately designed ruse to keep you under control and insecure for their purposes. Once you can accept that, then it's time to address the shame and self-blame that will inevitably occur, even though you are the victim of the situation.

Feel angry, feel sad, feel wretched, feel used. It is where you need to let all your emotions out in a catharsis instead of keeping them inside. Keeping them inside doesn't acknowledge them and keeps the truth from resonating within your heart and mind.

Third, you will need to reconnect with your life. The people, the work, the places, and find your place back within it. It is something that will not be without challenge, as your life and the world you left behind may not have changed too much, but you have. It may be a reverse culture shock to re-immerse yourself into normal life, so to speak, without inherent danger or abuse.

It may be difficult to remember how life was before abuse. You may not be able to trust people again. You may feel like your emotions need protection. However, it's a process, and little by little, you will discover that people won't betray your trust when you slowly open back up to them.

There are many lasting effects from an abusive relationship, but beyond the rain lies the rainbow.

17) Trauma Bond

It takes the step necessary to divorce the narcissist; it does not come easy. It becomes harder the longer you've been involved in the overvaluation phase of a relationship with a narcissist. There is a push and pull with narcissist's relationship that is all-consuming because despite how low this relationship, the highest will also be increased. Those highs are addictive.

The attachment that a victim feels to a narcissist despite knowing better is called a trauma bond. It is quite similar to Stockholm syndrome. A trauma bond is one that develops between a victim and an abuser. The abuser uses the victim's feelings of excitement, fear, emotional feelings, and sexual psychology to entangle them.

Victims of a narcissistic relationship developed codependency issues because they felt so loved and cared for initially. Even as these feelings erode over time and with the revelation of the narcissist's true nature, the emotional, mental attachment remains firm. While the victim might understand that the relationship structure has changed, she does not know why it occurs.

This lack of understanding makes her believe that if she tries to understand why the relationship is falling apart, she could take the steps necessary to get back to the relationship's love-bombing part. As a result, the victim finds it very difficult to enforce boundaries in the relationship. The weaker the victim's will of the enforcement becomes, the more complete the abuser's control.

The stronger a trauma bond is, the more likely the victim is to support the abuser's abusive behavior and the abuser's reasons for it. Because of this support, the victim develops negative feelings towards someone who tries to assist her in moving on.

How a Trauma Bond Develops

The development of the trauma bond is not magic. It is in science. Surviving any trauma activates a part of the brain known as the survival brain. It makes use of the part of the brain known as the amygdala. This part of the brain does not use reasoning skills or logic. It merely develops instinctive reactions to threats, and as such, the goal is simple - survival. This instinct is so strong that it suppresses logical decision-making to ensure that the victim survives the drama. This part of the brain releases hormones that enforce the bond, such as oxytocin, endogenous opioids, corticotropin-releasing factor, and dopamine.

One of the simplest yet most effective survival techniques is forming bonds with other people. There is safety in numbers. Most often, a narcissist will trap the victim into cutting ties with other people in their life. The narcissist becomes the only person in the victim's life, ensuring no one can form an attachment. The trauma bond ensures that the victim remains trapped in an endless cycle because the victim will stay in that relationship as a survival mode.

The victim is not thinking about the long-term implications of a relationship because her brain is only concerned with ensuring that the victim survives in the short run. For example, a woman who is being physically abused by a narcissist may feel that if she employs a long-term strategy like running away, then the narcissist may kill her compared to if she stays and endures, then she will survive. Because of this reasoning, the victims of narcissistic relationships develop a passive attitude towards being abused.

If the victim of a trauma bond finally does find the strength to walk away, the narcissist is cunning enough to switch tactics and cycles back to the first phase of a narcissistic relationship. It reawakens the brain's reward center and strengthens the trauma bond that the victim has developed.

Symptoms That You are Suffering from a Narcissistic Trauma Bond
Not sure if you display signs of a trauma bond? The symptoms listed below will help you figure it out:
- Receiving just a few crumbs of affection, love, and validation from the narcissist makes your day.
- Receiving even a little bit of the warranty and other positive emotions that the victim received in the first stage of the relationship puts them on cloud nine because the reward center is activated at the narcissist's will.
- Feeling stuck in the relationship and see no way out. Many times, it is not that the victim cannot physically leave. The intense longing to be close to the narcissist is what confines the woman to that relationship.
- Feeling that the narcissistic partner will be the only one to fulfill your needs, even though this person is not currently doing so.
- Worrying that your actions and words will set the narcissists off. Walking on eggshells around the narcissist is standard and a great sign of trauma bonding.
- Your brush off or excuse the narcissist's bad behavior, even when confronted by friends or family.
- You often feel there's a level of "prey-predator" within that relationship and that your vulnerabilities are being exploited
- You are aware that the narcissist is being deceived but still cannot say that the relationship ties.
- You feel shame at the things she had done, accepted, and endured in this relationship.

Reading these symptoms can be disheartened because victims of narcissistic relationships suffered from some, if not all, of these symptoms. You likely recognized yourself and your behaviors within these signs.

Do not despair, though. The trauma bond is hard to break, but it is not a possible task. The rest of this book is dedicated to helping you do just that.

Tactics for Dealing with and Severing a Narcissistic Trauma Bond
A trauma bond is likened to drug addiction because it gives euphoria feelings and then sucks them away. We know of instances where persons have

beaten drug addiction, so women who suffer from a trauma bond developed from narcissistic relationships have the same hope.

The hope is only facilitated by acting. There are methods that you can do to finally break free of that trauma bond that you have developed with your narcissistic husband. They include:

Taking it one day at a time. It is easy to become dumbfounded when making decisions about your future and moving on from a narcissistic relationship. It can make it seem easier to stick with the status quo. You cannot allow that to happen. Therefore, to ensure that you move on for good, make one decision, and move on one day.

You are committing to living in reality. The trauma bond is sustained by fantasies that things can be different and that a narcissistic partner can change. Remember that narcissism can only be dealt with by the narcissist. It would be best if you pulled yourself out of fantasies, deal with what is happening, and that this person is toxic to your health. The only reasonable response to that is getting rid of that toxicity.

You are living here and now. Many of the fantasies that sustained a trauma are founded on what could be and only do the narcissist outline. Stop that detrimental psychology by being aware of how you feel now and what is happening now. That is the only way you will notice that this person compromises your sense of self-worth and self-love. That will allow you to see the obvious that can stop being apparent. Stop waiting for a change and act on what is happening now.

Acknowledge your role in the narcissistic relationship. The narcissist would have placed all the blame on your shoulders for the things that went wrong. However, you need to back off a little and put things in perspective. If you were as bad as this person said, then he would have walked away. The point that he had not supported the fact that he was using you. Putting things in perspective allows you to see the obvious and break free of the emotional prison.

You are allowing yourself to feel. There are many messy emotions involved in being in a toxic relationship, and sometimes, it can seem more comfortable not to feel them. To be able to get past them is to handle them and acknowledge them for what they are. Then you can develop the techniques necessary to manage them healthily.

You are allowing yourself to grieve. By severing your trauma bond with a narcissist, you will enable this relationship to die. Grief is one of the critical phases for getting over any death or loss.

You are committing to self-care. Self-care is not just a physical endeavor. It is about emotionally and mentally caring for yourself as well. A narcissist will teach his victim to discard such personal caring. Therefore, to counter this, start making decisions that focus on your needs and wants. Thought about what is best for you, and the first step to doing that is compassionate and understanding towards yourself. Stop bothering yourself about your past decisions, and start encouraging yourself to uplift and empower yourself.

You are making a list of personal boundaries that must be honored by the other party if ever you'll be in a romantic relationship again. These boundaries are meant for both you and the other party. Limits can be simple, such as not entertaining a man who drinks heavily or not allowing someone else to control your finances no matter what. The point is that writing this will solidify them in your mind and, therefore, will enable you to recognize when another person is trespassing these boundaries.

You are developing a healthy support system. The narcissist may have achieved his goal of cutting the links that you had with other people. But this is the time in your life where you must commit to rebuilding old connections, healing from a trauma bond all the more difficult if you have no one around you to show you care and concern. If you do not have that ready support in your life, do not be afraid to reach out to a trained medical health professional.

You are allowing yourself to think of your life as bright and fulfilling without this person. Visualize having a supportive and uplifting partner rather than displaying behaviors that encourage a trauma bond development. Envision your life doing things as an individual so that even if your future does not have a romantic relationship, you will still be happy and fulfilled. Hold onto that vision and start implementing measures that will allow you to make it a reality. Such actions can include starting new hobbies, joining clubs, and furthering your education.

18) Avoid Repeating Errors after Leaving in a Toxic Relationship

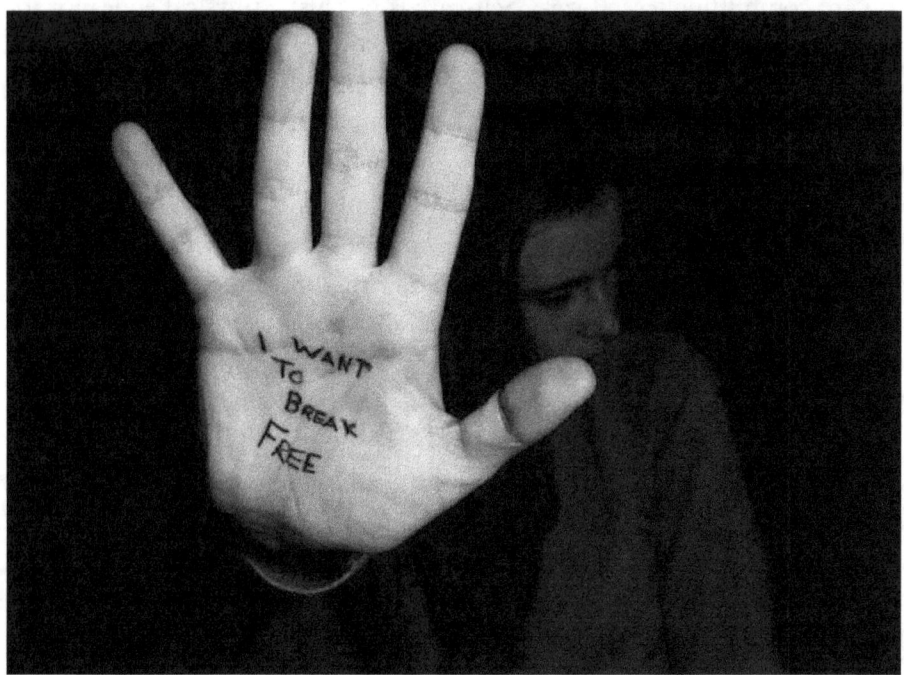

Narcissistic relationships are the most dangerous to go through, and one of the most difficult to escape. Recovery may take years, based on the abuse that was forced on you during the relationship. You have already learned what can and might happen through the official break-up, but recovery can be just as hard – if not more difficult than suffering through the actual break-up and its aftermath. Once we understand why it's so challenging to get over a narcissist, we can avoid the errors we have made in our recent toxic relationship.

Ordinary Things Were A Big Deal

As the narcissist took over our lives, they took over our minds. So, what was normal became abnormal due to their conditioning and their reasoning behind their abusive ways. We were screamed at for having friends of the opposite gender. We were blamed for telling the truth. We were punished for being honest. We were insulted for being vulnerable. Everything the narcissist put you through changed your way of thinking and, eventually, how you perceived the world.

They Controlled Every Aspect Of Our Lives

Did you feel trapped? Like you were walking on eggshells? Did you feel as if your voice and opinion didn't matter? Were your perception and beliefs changed by the countless times that you tried but weren't good enough? The narcissist gained complete control over you, your thoughts, your beliefs, and your personality. They made you question everything, to the point where you felt utterly crazy. For example, the narcissist might have tried to find any reason to accuse you of something you have not done, then lash out and threaten you over it. Now, you are going over everything and making sure nothing can be found, which only makes you seem guiltier and more suspicious. In a narcissist's eyes, you're always mistaken, and there will always be a problem.

We Justified Their Behavior

At the beginning of the relationship, you might have had firm boundaries and beliefs. You had perhaps set strict values and knew what you would put up with and what was not acceptable. Through your relationship, they pushed your limits, invaded your boundaries, and disrespected your space. As a result of these actions, you may have lashed out, acted differently than normal, and unleashed your inner beast in retaliation. It was ultimately determined to be your fault because they can do no wrong. It would be best if you forgave yourself for this, as you were in survival mode and your defense mechanisms come out. Your recovery is about understanding who you were, who you turned into, then escaping the nightmare to become who you want to be.

Our Realities Were Distorted

Through abuse tactics such as gaslighting, manipulation, and exploitation, the narcissist used against the things you said, saw, read, or what someone else said, saw, or read. But defending yourself led to thinking up ways to get back at them, and maybe even trying to do it; however, it only showed that you had something to hide. Their stories always seemed to change when you asked them about themselves, which would lead to an even bigger argument. Ever get out of the relationship and think, "I know nothing about them?" Your reality was distorted because you always had to tell them every detail about your life, how you were raised, and what brings you to the decisions you make now. We never knew who they were

Leaving The Relationship, You May Wonder If They Ever Loved You.
Did they ever care? What was their purpose in ruining your life? How was any of it fair? What did you do to deserve this? Why do they hate you so much? Why did they say they love you if they didn't show it? And they're a lot of questions more that will not be able to answer because the narcissist's behavior was all over the place and didn't make a whole lot of sense. One day, they were charming, sweet, innocent, and real with you, while then, they were utterly vindictive and evil. How were you to know what was real and what wasn't, with the constant whiplash in emotions?

Betrayal Became Part Of Our Worlds
A narcissist is good at gaining our trust to tell them things in confidence, then exploit what we told them as a way to use it against us. They may have lied, cheated, played games, or egged you on to get action out of you so that when you did, they could immediately turn around and play the victim card. It is called the trauma bond, where they push and pull, gain your respect, seduce you to blind you, then tug on your heartstrings and point out your weaknesses. After looking back on everything, now you feel betrayed, lost, hurt, and, worst of all, empty.

More Than The Relationship Was Lost
Like most relationships, you give yourself to someone expecting the same in return. When you break up, they seem to take that part of you with them, but you are relieved or almost grateful for it because you have grown. However, in a narcissistic relationship and break-up, you didn't willingly give yourself to them – they took it from you through their abusive nature, and you had no choice but to be vulnerable and try your hardest to keep the peace. When the relationship ended, they didn't just break up with you; they broke small parts of you everywhere.

Look back to what you had and who you were before ever meeting them. Now, look at who you are and what you have now.

Everything that you were and had is gone. It is challenging for most people to accept this reality and move on from this emotional and mental abuse. Outsiders or onlookers may have judged you, and you may have lost some friends along the way because of this relationship. No one truly understands a narcissist's "love" unless they have been in your shoes. You were blinded by seduction, given false hope along the way, and believed that they could do better. A way to rise above and recover from the relationship is to gain back others' support and start taking care of yourself.

How to Avoid Being Sucked Back In

A narcissist will try to 'hoover' their way back into your life by coming up with creative ways to get ahold of you or know what you are doing. In a way, you could call it a stalker-type way of trying to gain information on you to figure out if you still think of them. Here are some hoovers they will use and how to counteract them:

The Fake Emergency Hoover

The narcissist will often fake sickness or injury to get you to come to them or visit them in the hospital. They may go as far as actually hurting themselves to win you over. They may use a friend in their attempts as a proxy if you have cut all contact. Their sole intention behind their friend doing their dirty work is:

That you might not recognize or realize that the person is their friend, and you will feel more comfortable taking the bait if it's not directly from the narcissist.

As the information is not coming from the narcissist, it is easier to believe an outsider.

The empath will do more for someone who hasn't hurt them if the outsider seems to be in desperate need.

The best way to challenge or counteract this type of hoover method is to see it for what it is. If someone close to you talks about the narcissist all the time, they need some strict boundary rules. Kindly tell the people you know that you would not like to engage in any conversations that have to do with the narcissist – even if they are in the hospital or need.

The Reverse Hoover

This hoover speaks for itself. The narcissist lets it be known that they want nothing to do with you or your life. They say that they have moved on and that they are indeed through with you for good. However, the trick is that the narcissist says this to your friends, family, and people they know you are talking to. In a way, this is so they don't have to give you closure and that you will come running back to them demanding closure and asking questions. The narcissist knows that it is natural to want what you don't have and do what you can't do with any human being.

So, they play on this by letting "your people" know what they think of you – challenging you indirectly. When you run to them, they can deny that any of these rumors were said, thus welcoming you into their arms to supply their need for attention once more.

To counteract this, avoid acting on impulse or emotion, as the narcissist has no empathy. They want what they want, and if you feed into the rumors and go asking questions, they will suck you back in with their charm and persuasion. When you hear what has been said, convince yourself that what was said is real, and you don't need closure as you will take this opportunity to grow and finally heal.

The Psychic Connection

It will work on especially spiritual people. Maybe you have told the narcissist about your beliefs in astrology, telepathy, emotional bonds and connections, hidden communication with animals, etc. If you have, they will use this piece of information to their advantage. The narcissist will reach out to you through a letter or a "sign" that they set up and know only you would notice. This sign may lead you to think of them- maybe you made a spiritual bond when you were together. Now, every time you see this sign, it will trigger you to be with them.

The Silent Hoover

The silent hoover is the narcissist's way to give you your voice. They pretend to allow you closure but still don't give it to you.

Similar to the reverse hoover technique, the narcissist will reach out to the people around you and spread incredible rumors or lies so that you will come to them and speak your peace. An example of this is that the narcissist will post something on their social feed indiscreetly to get your attention, and only you or your friends would know it's about you. Then, as you find it insulting, you will need to reach out and explain what happened.

If you feel the need to clear yourself, only explain to the people who matter the most. Do not reach out to the narcissist, do not try to persuade them to remove the post; if you do, it will only cause conflict, and they will have sucked you back in by using the trauma bond to get inside your head again.

19) Professional and Medical advice from Narcissistic Abuse

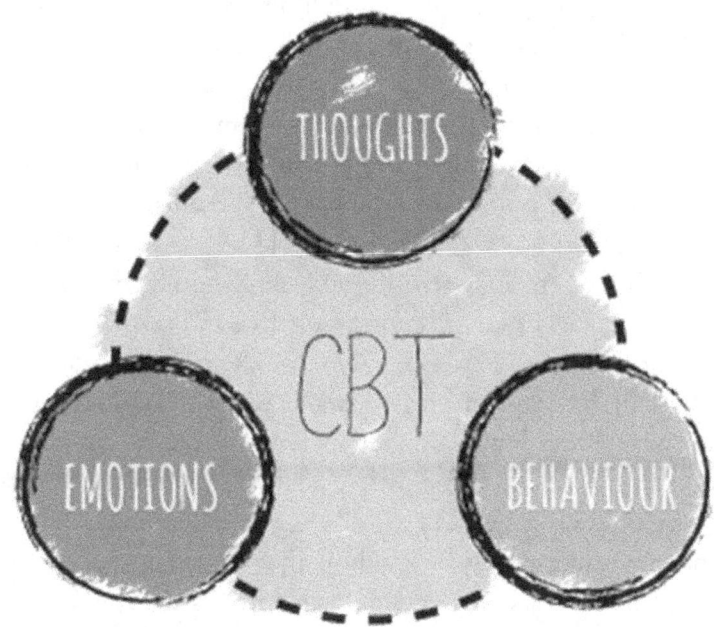

Below is the medical therapy for those who suffer from narcissistic abuse to speed their recovery and healing process:

Cognitive Behavioral Therapy (CBT)

A patient affected by narcissism often shows self-lost behavior, presenting signs of withdrawal from others, low self-esteem, fear of rejection, and negatives self-perception. These signs are strategies a patient employ to cope with the effect of past traumatic experiences or compensate for what was lost or denied. The copying strategies might cause more harm to the affected person. Cognitive-behavioral therapy aims to help the individual be affected by narcissism to change harmful copying-strategies and adopt strategies that gradually help the patient redeem. This method is not sometimes easy if the patient is not ready to open up and share the doctor's traumatic experiences. Therefore, the doctor should be more skilled in bringing the patient to feel comfortable to share the experiences.

It involves the doctor building trust and providing a friendly environment that lets the patient relieve emotions. In some instances, the patient does not understand why he or she shows certain behaviors, and the help of a person who was close during the traumatic experiences is needed. However, the patient must be comfortable with the third party during the therapy sessions. When the patient opens up, the doctor skillfully evaluates by questioning the events that have led to the client's present behavior. At this point, the session is meant to make the patient confront the past; it might be painful because it is like going through the traumatic events one more, but it helps the individual develop better strategies to overcome them positively.

After the confession of past events, the patient should suggest ways to forget the past. At this point, the doctor should be careful not to impose strategies that the patient is not comfortable, but should give guidance to make sure that the suggestions are more adaptive and positive. Cognitive Behavioral therapy is not time-bound, because the progress from one stage to another or length of a given stage depends on the patient; the essential aspect is the internal resolution and reconciliation of the past and the present. The main goal is that the patient achieves an inner balance and discovers himself and herself. There is also a sense of compassion, which helps the patient understand why and how the past events happened. This stage is also meant to make the patient develop skills such as self-regulation and resilience.

When the patient is strong enough to face the problem and develops strategies to cope with the doctor's guidance, the negative behaviors are slowly faced and replaced with positive coping behaviors. There is a need for continuous observation of the patient during the behavior change process to reduce fall back chances. Also, those close to the patient should be guided to help the patient during recovery.

Eventually, the patient corrects the people's faulty interpretations and the environment and replaces them with more rational and accurate performances. Therefore, the patient can understand that the environment gives what you give it and starts to engage in behavior that gives more positive experiences leading to stable behavioral and emotional reactions that are not harmful and exaggerated.

DBT (Dialectical Behavior Therapy)

It is more like focus groups but is conducted by a therapist and involves sharing the past with others. Therapy is also highly recommended by psychologists as one way of dealing with narcissistic abuse. A narcissist can leave one in a lousy stage that can cause brain damage or losing their minds. Seeing a therapist and opening up to someone who can understand and guide you to recovery is paramount. A behavioral therapist can organize a small group of her patients and do live coaching to help them know that what they are going through is nothing different from others and work collectively to bettering their lives.

After narcissistic abuse, one does not feel the need to be with people. They often cut communications; having a behavioral group can help them come back to normal and trust a few people. There are three types of DBT that a therapist might find it necessary for their patients.

Meditation

Meditation is a recommended technique that helps one to focus on something for soul searching and relaxation. Meditation is a homemade skill that can help one redeem themselves after a bad day or bad experience. Meditation is the skill of the mind and training it to behave in a particular manner

Yoga

It is the physical training of the mind. Unlike meditation, Yoga prepares both the body and mind and helps in recollecting self from the broken pieces caused by a narcissist. Someone who has gone through narcissist abuse is always paranoid and is not taking care of themselves, which is more destructive than narcissism itself. Through Yoga, one can reclaim their bodies and state of mind by practicing ways to have a weakness. Monks in a temple were among the first people to realize Yoga to reconnect themselves with the inner being. For recovery after suffering from abuse, Yoga is the best remedy.

Support Groups

It is not a professional way of getting help, but it reduces the burden on one's mind. They say problems shared is half solved. Unlike group therapy, the Support group is run entirely by members going through the same experience with the rest.

Support Group is essential for someone who just got out of narcissistic abuse in a relationship or family. It helps connect with others who went through the same or even worse scenario and came out strong like never before. Many of popular support groups are health-related because diseases drain energy. It could be cancer, AIDS, and other deadly diseases. Narcissistic abuse is also a disorder that affects the brain, thus the importance of the support group. Everyone in our lives may not connect with you because they do not know what you are going through and might not give the best care you deserve. In support groups, everyone shares their experience in narcissism-filled family or relationships. The opening up to total strangers also eases one's pain and help recollect of the human part that was lost in deep thoughts that at some point, are suicidal.

20)   Your Road to Recovery

Recovery is for those who have been through abuse. If you have been in a relationship with a narcissist, it is high time you left and sought help from a professional—this kind of support you need to rebuild your self-confidence and bounce back to your self-esteem.

Trust me; you are better than you have ever thought possible. The narcissist might have managed to puncture your self-confidence and even crush your self-esteem, but most importantly, you are just a victim. You are not unworthy like they want you to believe. Finding a health professional with a specialty in trauma recovery will help you journey through the healing process to recovery. Suppose you are not able to leave the relationship. In that case, a therapist can also help you learn the best ways to communicate effectively with your abuser to set boundaries that they will respect and hence, protect you so that they will no longer take advantage of you.

Below are paths that you need to go through to help you journey through healing to recovery:

Step 1: Cut Contact
Once you have left the relationship, keep it at that! Stop maintaining contact with your abuser. The main reason why you left is that the situation was not working for you. Therefore, there is nothing that will happen that can make things better. The best way to recover from abuse is for you to block all forms of communication.

If your co-parenting children, you may not wipe this person entirely from your life. Therefore, it is advisable to create a strict custom contract, according to which you only communicate on matters regarding your children using third-party channels exclusively! Otherwise, ensure that you have set up court orders for all forms of agreements.

Think about the extreme trauma bonding, the gross abuse, and the addiction you had with the narcissist. Sometimes the best way is for you to accept that the only way you can recover from such damage is to pull away and cut your losses once and for all. Think of abstaining as a way of protecting yourself from hurt. In other words, each time you initiate contact with your abuser, you are handing them the ammunition to blow you off.

Remember that you lived with them and so they know what your weak points are and how they can wound you even more profoundly. It is not until we heal that we will stop forcing ourselves on the narcissist for love or craving them or even justifying to ourselves, giving them a second chance. When we completely stop contact, then we can begin to heal.

Step 2: Release That Trauma So That You Begin Functioning Again
If we are going to heal, we have to be willing to reclaim our power. We have to do the exact opposite of what we used to believe; "I can fix him, I will feel better." Your power belongs inside you. When you don't focus away from your abuser, you will be able to channel that power into rebuilding your self-love and paying closer attention to making yourself whole again. At first, it might seem like understanding who a narcissist is and what they do is essential. These things cannot heal your internal trauma. Decide to let go of that horrific experience so that you can be at peace. You will begin to rise, get relief, and balance again once you have decided to take your power where it belongs-inside you.

Step 3: Forgive Yourself

When the insecure and wounded parts of us are still in pain, we often are pushed into behaving like children who are damaged. We are continually looking for people's approval, and especially from our abuser, we hand our abuser the power to treat us as they see fit. And that's the time you will realize that you have given them all your resources: money, time, and health. The most unfortunate thing is that while doing that, you end up hurting the people that matter the most in your life, your children, siblings, parents, and friends.

Yes, it might be hard to forgive yourself for this, but you can do that if you want to rebuild your life and everything you lost to your abuser. By working through your healing process, you will soon find resolution and acceptance. You can move away from lacking self-love and respect to living a life full of truth, responsibility, and well-being.

You will realize that, when you forgive yourself, you acknowledge that this was all a learning curve, and this is the experience you learned, and hence, you will use that to reclaim your life. When you release your regrets and self-judgments, you can start setting yourself free to realize your life's greatness, irrespective of what stage you are at. It is the point when you will begin to feel hope again, hope that will steer you forward into fulfillment and a life full of purpose.

Step 4: Release Everything And Heal All Your Abuser's Fears And What They Might Do Again

Do you know what bait to a narcissist is? Anxiety, pain, and distress. These are the things that can perpetuate another cycle of abuse, no matter how we tell ourselves that we have separated from them. It is indeed true that abusers can be relentless. In most cases, they do not like being losers. You have to realize that they are not as powerful and impactful as you may have thought them to be.

They need you to fear and go through pain so that they can function. Once you have healed your emotional trauma, they fall apart. Therefore, you must become grounded and stoic by not feeding into their drama; this way, they will soon wither away and their power and credibility.

Step 5: Release The Connection To Your Abuser

So many people have likened their freedom from a narcissist to that of exorcism. When we liberate ourselves from the darkness that filled our beings, we allow ourselves to detox and let light and life come in. In the same manner, you must release all the parts that your abuser trapped so that you can tap into a more supernatural power, the power of pure creativity. When you disentangle yourself from the narcissist, it is not just about cutting the cord; it is also about releasing all the belief systems you might have associated yourself with subconsciously. Only then can you break free to be a new person and not a target of a narcissist.

Even though it might be tempting to seek revenge on your abuser, this is something that you have to try hard to avoid. Rage has the power of pulling you back into deeper darkness and a game that your abuser is an expert in the first place. The best form of revenge is one in which you decide to take back your freedom and render your abuser irrelevant.

And it is likely going to crush their ego, and they will be powerless and at a loss that they cannot even affect you. Often, they are in despair when it hits that you are a constant reminder of their extinction. This end and your soul contracts to allow love and healing so that you can be whole again.

Step 6: Realize Your Liberation, Truth, And Freedom

Traditionally, we learn that loving ourselves is a very selfish act. However, when it comes to finding liberation and freedom from our abusers' hands, it is a critical step that allows us to take in the truth and let it set us free from captivity. Yes, it is incredibly challenging to do, but it is a necessary step toward achieving liberation.

Society has taught us that we are treated by others the same way we treat them. However, this is a false premise because we get treatment according to the way we treat ourselves. In other words, the measure of love that we obtain from others is equivalent to that we feel about ourselves.

Therefore, when we open up to healing and recovery, we open the doors for others to love us in reality and in more healthy ways than ever before. This act serves as a template by which we teach our children not to carry around subconscious patterns of abuse passed by our ancestors.

This positive modeling only starts when we decide to take responsibility for our happiness and freedom. We slowly become the change that we would wish to see to let go of being someone's victim and stop handing other people our power.

In other words, we take back our lives by doing everything necessary to aid our inner healing irrespective of what the narcissist does or does not do, something that's now irrelevant either way. At this point, we can thrive despite what we have been through and what has happened to us.

So, what do you need to learn?

Refocus

When you let go, you will be able to experience the power that comes with healing. Take time to release those bonds to your abuser so that you can refocus all of your efforts on building yourself and a new life.

Self-Confidence

If you live a life of greatness after your abuse, you must be willing to start putting back your life together. You have to come out with self-confidence so that you can reclaim your old self and find an even higher power to steer you forward towards success and victory. Once you start experiencing self-love, it is then that you will be able to turn a chaotic life into one that has calmness and joy.

Willingness To Transition Your Relationships Into Mature And Real Levels Of Intimacy

The good thing about having survived abuse is the fact that you are empathetic. In other words, you learn what it takes to experience a healthy relationship filled with love and care for the other person. It is with this understanding that you will be able to exercise self-awareness. You will be interested in truly knowing the other person well on a deeper, more personal level so that you can unravel their real personality.

However, the good thing is that even as you heal and move on with your life, you will spot a narcissist by the fact that they cannot grow their relationships into mature levels. They, therefore, remain stuck in cycles of devaluation.

As a survivor, you are better equipped to move on past your pain and abuse to having a healthy relationship, whether in your family, workplace, or love.

21) Allowing Yourself to Be Who You Are

The last part of your road to recovery is allowing yourself to be who you are. Who you are is a combination of you were before, are right now, and where you would like to be in the future. Who you were when you were in a relationship with a narcissist might feel distant from you now, but this experience is part of you now.

You might not have felt like yourself for a while, but you have always been you.

Therein lies the main difference between who you were then, and you want to become. You want to become comfortable with yourself again, right? That's the final goal for your recovery.

The following activities are geared to maintain the progress of your recovery. It helped you reclaim your identity and maintain a level of comfort with the identity you have begun to establish.

Separate Your Identity from the Narcissist

Do not try to continue running in the same circles as the narcissist. Find new friends. Separate from the narcissist as possible. You might have family ties, divorce, or custody considerations about this. Of course, there may be circumstances that do not allow for your separation.

Yet, it would be best if you separated in the ways you can. You will need to ask yourself if your identity is still bound to the narcissist in any way. It would be best if you kept adding to your identity. The critical aspect of these new additions regarding your recovery is that these new additions separate you from the narcissist. They should not pull you backward. They should push you forward.

Find Something That Makes You Feel Strong

The point is that you pursue some activity that will make you healthier and make you feel confident. Strength will help you maintain your recovery. Strength will keep you motivated. Strength will keep you from relapsing. Find some activity that you pursue for a length of time that will make you stronger in whatever way you deem valuable.

Be Extremely Honest and Upfront

It will help you maintain your sense of self. It will also help you avoid dishonesty in your upcoming relationship.

Be as honest as you want someone to be with you. Be upfront about who you are. You are angered at the fact that the narcissist you were with hid their true selves from you. Don't hide your true self from the people you meet. Be the person you want to be and be honest about who that person is. Undo the narcissist's cognitive dissonance in which a person's image matters more than the actual person. Be more than an image, be honest, real, and be you.

Be Assertive

If you've managed to be honest and upfront, you can manage to be assertive. The difference is simply the confidence behind your honesty. Assertive means you're self-assured. Being proactive means you have been honest with yourself, and you know what you think about something.

An assertive person has undeniable confidence because they aren't at odds with themselves. They know what they're saying. They believe they're right to say it.

The big difference is that you should know you deserve what you have asked for. A narcissist often thinks they have been wronged in some way because they don't already have what they deserve. Someone assertive knows that they don't just get to have things, but they are willing to fight back for themselves when they realize they have been cheated.

Be Outgoing

Part of establishing yourself and being you have to be done in front of and with others. There are many ways in which your recovery can take place in isolation, but at some point, you need to go out and meet new people who can observe you as you are right now. The narcissist you were with was probably jealous when you were particularly outgoing and attracted more attention than they did. You may have held yourself back for their sake. It's time to be outgoing again.

They are no longer an excuse to hold you back. Get out there and get attention. The narcissist probably made you feel ashamed if you took care away from them, but they cannot shame you anymore.

Be outgoing and perhaps even flirtatious. You will feel better once you find yourself able to go out and feel attractive again without worrying that you're hurting the narcissist's feelings. The point is not to become the town spectacle, but a little bit of fun will be good for you.

A little bit of attention will be healthy for you. A little bit of flirting will be just fair. Enjoy yourself. Make yourself enjoy being outgoing in a way you have not in however long it has been.

Try New Things

Part of the abuse of being with a narcissist is the feeling of being stuck. Narcissists get stuck quickly because of their entitlement and their avoidance of reality. Trying current things will keep you from feeling stuck again. You might need to try a lot of new things at first. Eventually, you'll have recovered enough to settle back into a routine of some kind.

Until then, you might want to try something new daily, weekly, or as needed. Any time you feel stuck in a way that reminds you of how you felt when you were with a narcissist, you should go out and try something new.

In any case, trying new things will help you maintain your sense of identity. We learn new things about ourselves when we try new things. Anytime you feel the need to learn something about yourself, try something new. It will always do the trick.

Do Volunteer Work

Volunteer work is an incredible way to learn about yourself and feel good about yourself while stepping away from yourself. You step away from yourself when you volunteer because you are doing something for someone else.

You might think this kind of work would be counterproductive because you have been volunteering your efforts to the narcissist for so long, but it will feel good to place the same type of effort elsewhere.

Combine your self-love and other-love now. Being with a narcissist is that your love was going into a leaky vessel. You kept giving it, and it was received, but it never filled either of you up. The reason for this is the leak. A narcissist's love capacity is like a leaky vessel because it is tough to feel before it gets emptied again. You worked hard, but it didn't always yield the same result. Sometimes you were appreciated.

Narcissists know a little about positive reinforcement. Other times, you were not so successful. Volunteer work should be more fulfilling work than the work you did for the narcissist. Sure, it may never feel as good as it thought those few glorious times when the narcissist gave you the recognition you deserved, and it's true.

A narcissist can make you feel outstanding about the work you did for them. There's no denial about that to be found in this book. Still, since the narcissist struggled enough to appreciate you that you have diagnosed them as a narcissist, then volunteer work will be a more reliable source of fulfillment than the narcissist was in your relationship.

Be Humble, but Don't Minimize Your Accomplishments

Being humble is tied to honesty and reality. It would be best if you stayed humble to maintain the success of your recovery. Getting too proud or boastful will not do you any favors. Be honest with yourself about your mistakes. Be honest with yourself about your successes.

Likely, you were excessively hard on yourself for your relationship with a narcissist, and you minimized your successes. Now you do not have to do either of those things anymore.

You may acknowledge your mistakes without feeling an abundance of shame. Feel a realistic amount and then move forward. Acknowledge that the amount of shame the narcissist you were with made you think for a mistake was outrageous. Feel the amount of shame you think someone else should feel for that mistake and then move on to the upcoming thing you have to do.

Don't minimize your accomplishments, either. Allow yourself an amount of celebration that you would deem appropriate for someone else. Think about what amount of celebration you think an achievement of that sort deserves and then grant yourself dessert of such a celebration.

Take Yourself to Dinner

It would be great for you to reward yourself for your work. If you think about what makes you stick with a fitness routine or a diet, the answer is probably the result. Reward yourself for your recovery. Take yourself out to dinner. Take yourself somewhere new and exciting.

Treat yourself to a little vacation. Reward yourself for taking steps toward your recovery. Think about how often you indulged the narcissist you were within rewarding themselves. Go ahead and give yourself a turn.

Taking yourself out to dinner is a sign of self-assurance. It takes confidence to go out to dinner simply because you feel you deserve it. You might not want to go alone. That's fine. Bring someone along. The point is that you reward yourself for doing good work. You deserve an appreciable reward for your work. Sure, recovery is rewarding enough. Even so, you are more likely to maintain your recovery status if you are giving yourself positive affirmation for all of the work you have done to be right where you are.

Keep a Record of Your Work

Not only should you reward yourself, but you should also keep a record of your work. It might even help you mark your success in a way that makes you more confident that you do, indeed, deserve your reward. In other words, you can write down the activities you think would be practical work for you.

Then, you can write down the kind of reward you think you deserve to complete each activity. Then, you will not be stuck questioning whether or not you deserve a reward for your work or not. You will already have decided what your rewards should be for specific work and specific activities.

It is essential to see what you have done to feel proud of your work and motivated to continue it. One benefit of having a personal trainer for fitness has that trainer record your results. It is essential for any regime that a record is kept. Otherwise, you will be unable to assess your progress. Keep a record in some fashion. Keep a journal. Post the positive affirmations you maintain on social media. Whatever suits your style is the right way to record your work. The point is that you find some way to measure your progress to appreciate it.

Remember, you deserve to appreciate your accomplishments. Don't minimize anything about yourself anymore. Be who you are.

Be proud of yourself. Be honest about your accomplishments. It includes celebrating the ones worth celebrating.

22)   Loving Again

So, you've begun to recover from your relationship with a narcissist, and you're ready to move forward. You can set the terms of a relationship to some extent, and the start is the best time to do it. You will have to think about your patterns, and you will be feeling fresh and energized and ready for dating again.

5 Early Signs you've Finally Found a Good Partner
Finding someone who is going to make your world a happier place, not turn it upside down. Here is an indication to look out for when you start dating that will signal you've found someone you are compatible with.

You Feel Physically At Ease In Their Presence
 If you're with someone right for you, who isn't going to harm you, you will probably get a warm and comfortable feeling. The conversation will flow smoothly most of the time. You won't find yourself worrying about what you've said or done, and you will be enjoying yourself.
You'll feel physically safe, comfortable, and relaxed. Look for those feelings when you start dating and believe in them, even if the person isn't

necessarily your dream partner in every way — sometimes, it happens that way.

You Share Common Interests And Concerns

No matter how charming someone is, there needs to be more than just chemistry in a long-term relationship. If you feel that you share some similar interests and passions, it's a great compatibility sign. It does not mean someone who agrees with everything you say. It's more about sounding out your world view and knowing pretty quickly that the other person in on the same page.

It's great to have some areas where you have absolutely nothing in common. Someone with different interests can teach you about things you've never found interesting before. On the other hand, having interests that your partner doesn't share gives you a sense of space and maintains a separate identity.

Keep in mind that it's good to enjoy time off in the same way. If you love traveling and your prospective partner does not own a passport, a lifelong relationship may not be in the cards. If they are hugely invested in a hobby — cycling, gaming, running — that doesn't interest you at all, you might need to manage your expectations about their availability.

But if you find that you enjoy at least some of the same things — then chances are you'll enjoy each other's company.

They Always On Time

Narcissists are great at running late, creating drama with last-minute cancellations and let-downs. They make a great deal of fuss around the simple act of gracing you with their presence. It's not surprising that being around them can feel hectic and stressful.

What does the opposite experience look like? If someone shows up on time, looking friendly and relaxed, and you have an excellent time together — talking, chatting, walking, seeing a movie, or just enjoying a coffee together — you can start to let down your guard and relax.

When you start seeing someone, it should feel like getting to know a friend or work colleague more than a scene straight out of a Hollywood movie. It should feel relaxed, comfortable, fun. You should feel curious and enlivened, not overwhelmed or swamped with emotion and chemistry. There should be some chemistry, yes, but it shouldn't feel too urgent or over-the-top.

They are consistently kind and interested in you

Remember when we looked at intermittent reinforcement? The opposite of this is consistency. If someone is nice to you, but only sometimes, my advice would be to back off. But if someone is consistently pleasant and kind — not over the top, just decent — then you may well be in a keeper's presence. Don't waste time on someone who is only available sometimes, or who gives you just the crumbs of their attention. Generally, if someone likes you, you know it. It's not a mystery. If you find yourself wondering about where you stand with someone, likely, you aren't their top priority.

You Share Similar Lifestyles

Sleep, food, exercise, levels of tidiness, and daily habits such as reading or exercising — all of these mundane things make up the way you live your life. If you see some compatibility in the small things, then that is a perfect sign for your future together. If you walk into someone's house and like the way it looks and feels (rather than feeling impressed, awed, or just slightly nonplussed), you should trust that feeling. A long-term relationship isn't about mind-blowing passion and chemistry. It's about enjoying your daily life together, and your daily habits are a big part of this.

On this note, if you want to make your life easier, pay attention to how someone presents themselves and their living space. If they appear uncared for or chaotic, that should give you pause. And if that person is dependent on alcohol or other substances, be aware that they may not have the resources to be a good partner.

8 Great Habits to Start Your New Relationship the Right Way

Slow And Steady

Hold back when you meet someone new. Remember, if they are the ones, you have all the time in the world to enjoy that fact. If they are not, you should enjoy the relationship for what it is and protect yourself so you don't find yourself having to heal and recover from a disastrous relationship.

Treat Them Kind

Set the tone for the relationship you would like to have with someone by being that person yourself. Be kind. Be on time. Communicate as clearly as you can. A new relationship is a fresh start, and you can steer it in the right direction by being respectful and positive.

Even when arguments come along — and they will — remember that you have something special between you, and you need to look after that, even if you are having a temporary disagreement. It's possible to fight with someone while remaining respectful and not permanent damage to the bond between you.

If it's meant to be, you'll have set the groundwork for a rich and loving relationship by treating your partner as you would like to be treated.

Focus On The Other Person

It's often the result of many daily interactions, and learning to focus on someone and respond to them is a useful skill for any relationship, not just a romantic one.

To do this, first of all, eliminate distractions. Make time to spend with your partner, switch off screens, listen, and focus. Even if you are busy and rushing off in separate directions, eye contact and affection can help maintain a healthy and loving connection into the future.

Look After Yourself

Just because you've met someone new, this doesn't give you an excuse to stop your healing efforts from your experience with a narcissist. Keep doing all those things you did to recover — talking to a therapist, looking after your physical and mental wellbeing, journaling, and spending time alone to rest and recharge. Taking time out to reflect on where the relationship is going and how you feel is another way of looking after yourself as you move forward.

Even in the early days, get in the habit of setting aside some personal space, even if you feel like being with them all the time. Give them time to miss you and feel curious about what you've been up to. It's important to give yourself time to enjoy your own company.

Don't Dwell In The Past

Whatever happened with the narcissist, don't let yourself stay too much on it if it makes you feel bad. Spend some time with a therapist, but don't live there. When you find yourself ruminating or wondering how the narcissist is going, bring yourself firmly back into the present with self-care or distraction.

On this note, don't assume that all of your future partners will let you down. If you have made some effort on yourself and reflected on what may have led you to your narcissistic partner, you should be able to avoid carrying this baggage into your new relationship. Give this new person a chance.

Remembering How Far You've Come

You've been through quite an experience. Remember that you got yourself away, you are now safe, and you have a lot to look forward to.

If you find yourself regretting the time you spent with them, remind yourself that you have a whole future ahead of you that they no longer have the power to ruin. You are safe. You deserve to be happy.

Don't Badmouth The Relationship To Others

If you start with someone, it's sometimes a good idea to let it grow in its own time, and in private, before you start talking about it too much to others. It's natural to want to share your new relationship with friends and be mindful of how much you share. Try to keep some things private. There are reasons for this:

First, letting others into your new world with this person too quickly, mainly if they prefer you single, can hurt the new relationship. Secondly, talking about the relationship in detail with others has a way of taking away energy from its growth and opening up the unique bond you have formed to others' influence.

If you aren't sure about how it's going but generally feel OK, talk to your new partner, your journal, or your therapist. And if you think suddenly upset, don't go rushing off to badmouth your new partner to your friends. A new relationship is fragile, like a seedling or tiny baby, and you need to treat it well as it grows stronger.

Laugh Together

Sharing humor is one of the best ways to relieve stress and bond with your partner. And it's what makes being in a relationship with someone so much fun. So, don't forget to laugh, enjoy each other's company, and be silly together.

A Final Word On Finding New Love

As you move on from the narcissist, remember to be positive and hopeful for the future and realistic. Unfortunately, some people out there need to steer well clear of for your wellbeing and happiness. But many others will enrich your life. Ultimately, it's about finding that sweet spot between keeping yourself safe and trusting in those that you meet to do the right thing by you.

If the relationship you've had with a narcissist is good for anything, it's that you have learned how to look after yourself in all sorts of new ways. Believe in your new insights, get out there, and have fun!

Conclusion

After divorcing your relationship with a narcissist, it is easy to see how much we have changed and diverted from these relationships with the people that we need to have around us. We eject ourselves away from them because we have been manipulated into doing so, the narcissist continuing in their need for supply, seeing how far we will go for them and how much we love them. They make us fear that they can and will quickly leave us if we do not comply with their rules and stipulations. But once we are free from this, we can honestly create a safer environment where we can return to old relationships or develop new ones.

Reclaiming Your Reality
Forgive yourself and seek reminders of who you are. It is another time-consuming process and should never be rushed. Don't allow so-called friends and family members guilt you into "getting over it"; this is especially true for men recovering from abuse. Tell those who would push too hard to take a hike. It is an essential first step in recovering yourself. You were a healthy, capable person once, and you will be again.
Here are ways you can reclaim your reality:

Redefining Your Belief System
Understand that a part of you knew that abuse was happening, and don't think less of yourself because of it.
Most people do not abuse others. Most people out there who would never dream of hurting you, who at the very least would show you a minimum of respect and, at the most, would love you for the person you are, not the shadow they wish to torment. What you're doing now is strengthening yourself, so you can once again believe that there's a bright future waiting for you ahead. Remember, take this process one step at a time, and don't feel as if you're not making the process fast enough.

Rebuilding Your Trust
You will realize that part of you knew what was going on while you were with your abuser, and that will hurt. That will feel like a metric ton of shame, but you have to process it. All of us want to be happy; we want to love; we

want joy. You were holding out for that, but it never came. It is not your fault.

Re-Establishing Emotional Connection

It is for both the re-establishing of inner and external emotional connections you need to thrive again. As we know, life is entwined and made up of relationships, attachments, feelings, and emotions. They are the driving force behind all that we do. And to have these valuable assets in life, we can gain access to untapped mental well-being.

When we have removed ourselves from the narcissistic relationship, we need to re-establish our emotional connectivity. It is paramount to moving forward. All of this is related to the healing process that we need to go through. By re-establishing our emotional connection with someone or more than one person, we are continually moving further and further away from the relationship or friendship that we had with a narcissist who we loved and cared about.

Learning to Be Smart & Patient Through Experience

Being smart when moving forward can be quite fulfilling, knowing that we acknowledge our past experiences and can utilize this tool when trying to figure out what we need to avoid when healing. Knowing your limits and boundaries is vital. And it can be quite enlightening when making decisions. Being patient requires a lot of effort and mental strength. Often, we can forget this and demand ourselves to "forget" our experience with a narcissist. This process does happen quickly; there will still be that lingering attachment to them and feelings that are painful reminders.

We need to be educated from our experiences and to be patient with ourselves when we are healing. It can be highly frustrating as if the walls are seemingly closing in on us and running out of time. But the walls are not closing in on us, and we are not running out of time. Gradually, we will be able to get closer to where we want to be. If we follow the direction that we have chosen for ourselves while keeping in line with the boundaries that we have set, we can slowly guide ourselves to where we want to be.

Taking Steps Towards Loving Again

Heal your inner child. Reclaim your joy. Look at relationships in a balanced, healthy way. To start, you will need to shift your focus away from the concept of love for a while. It might seem counterintuitive, but you have a lot of rebuilding to do. Imagine a house that had caught fire but was mostly recovered. Would that house be suitable for someone to live in right away? No, it would need reconstruction and renovation. After dealing with a narcissist, you need that too.

A shift of focus can be anything from a new job, a hobby group, acquiring a new pet, or volunteering in some capacity at a non-profit, soup kitchen, or humane society.

Finally, you will need a lot of restraint. You will not be rebuilt in a day, just like that famous Italian city. Your healing and recovery will take time, as much time as it needs, and you are worth every minute it takes.

Being Happy Again
We have been knocked down, and now we are almost back at the top. We have regained our lives and developed self-awareness, self-love, and we have stayed within the boundaries that we have set for ourselves. We feel good and healthy, and we are noticing the positive changes that we have gone through. We are right there, and we deserve that. Being happy is a feeling that can set us in motion to newer and greater heights. We have overcome the state we were in, and now we are feeling good about how things have turned out, and with that, we are feeling good about ourselves.

But what does it take to become happy? The answer is simple: by accepting your past and experiences and understanding that you alone can shape and share your life with people who love you and want to be there for you. You have overcome abuse, degradation - you have healed in a sense that you now feel normal again.

We cannot merely find happiness without implementing the tools that are required to find happiness. It is difficult, and stubbornness is unleashed from within us, but that is good. It shows that we are not happy with who we were in the narcissistic relationship and feel the need to change and feel ourselves again.

www.ingramcontent.com/pod-product-compliance
Lightning Source LLC
Chambersburg PA
CBHW070920080526
44589CB00013B/1378